Value Forward Selling

HOW TO SELL TO MANAGEMENT

Become a peer in the boardroom...
instead of a vendor waiting in the hallway!

Paul R. DiModica

Publisher's Note

Second Edition.

International Standard Book Number: 1-933598-31-X

Published by Johnson & Hunter, Inc.
(www.johnsonhunter.com)

Trademarks

Bulk Sales

Johnson & Hunter offers excellent discounts on this book when ordered in quantity for bulk purchases or special sales. For more information, please contact **corpsales@johnsonhunter.com.**

Dedication

This publication and course
is dedicated to Renee, my
wife and business partner.
Without her unflagging
support, invaluable advice,
and extensive contribution,
this book would not have
been possible. Through her,
I have seen the possibilities.

Table of Contents

Preface

Dear Sales Professional,

Thank you for investing in my book and training course. I specialize in value forward marketing and sales strategy formation and sales training to help companies and individual salespeople market and sell products and services to management.

Throughout the last twenty years, I have sold millions of dollars of products and services to management teams of all sizes, from Fortune 100 firms to presidents of small privately held companies. I have competed against Fortune 500 sales organizations, high-priced consulting firms, low-cost providers, regional reseller players, wholesalers, aggressive startups, and companies that are dominant in their vertical spaces. But size doesn't matter. **Selling to management is a premeditated sport**. With consistent practice, you can prepare for the big game and, on any given Sunday, more times than not, you can beat any rival.

Today, most companies pull their value behind them and force their company into a commodity position with their competitors.

When sales executives say, "we have great service," "we are customer centric," or "our offerings are the best," - they just sound like their competition.

When you market and sell like your competitors - you become identical to your competitors . . . and you have to price your product or service equal to or less than your competitors.

To grow your firm in this market, you need to integrate your sales, marketing, and strategy programs into one outbound revenue capture approach focused on communicating your business value up front so prospects see you differently than your competition.

I developed Value Forward Selling™ based on personal experiences as a sales executive and company founder, as well as working with thousands of salespeople and doing sales and marketing strategy consulting with hundreds of companies.

Value Forward Selling focuses on a premeditated approach in which sales, marketing, and strategy are integrated into one outbound-revenue capture program. This book trains salespeople of all experience levels how to **become a peer in the boardroom, instead of a vendor waiting in the hallway.**

Simple concept—important sales approach.

It doesn't matter if your business is a one-person startup, a Fortune 1000 player, a family run business, or a national consulting company. If you sell any type of product or service and you currently sell to management or are trying to sell to management, this publication is for you.

If you are a salesperson, you have a sales quota (or target) that must be reached. If you are a business owner, you need to generate revenue to maintain your cash flow. Regardless of your position, the shortest path to increasing sales is by focusing on the best techniques, intelligent lead-generation marketing methods, and best practices to sell to management. And if you are a company sales manager who supervises a direct sales force, the number of salespeople you are responsible for only multiplies your frustration.

As a salesperson, I've constantly been exposed to market walls that tried to prevent me from meeting my quotas. As a result, I developed a specific methodology based on best practices of how to sell to management. This program teaches you how to quickly, efficiently, and profitably sell services and products of all types through the business impediments that stand in your way. If you implement this program's methods and techniques, you will have a *sales behavioral change* in how you sell.

In a world where competition erodes market share and depresses pricing, and where branding and marketing tramples the startup or small business owner, **the key is not *first* to market, but *smart* to market.**

To be honest, I have spent a dominant amount of my marketing, sales, and sales management career working with firms that were aggressively pursuing very competitive markets. The "David versus Goliath" scenario was a constant reality for me. In addition to working hard, I always had to work smarter. Some firms I worked with were startup companies with minimal revenue, entrenched competitors, and no clear market differentiation. Others were mature players with little funding for marketing and advertising. No matter what kind of product or service you sell, by the time you finish reading Value Forward Selling, you will have obtained the knowledge needed to become more successful, increase your income, grow your company, increase your wealth, and accelerate your career.

Value Forward Selling requires salespeople to become outbound Hunters—salespeople who proactively hunt for business and are knowledgeable about full sales cycles. Conversely, many salespeople are Farmers—salespeople who wait for corporate to give them leads and passively work a pipeline of existing customers. Through our techniques, we will teach you how to become a Hunter who sells more.

As you go through this book, I recommend you highlight areas that are important to you. Each chapter provides specific *action steps* to help you personalize Value Forward Selling to your marketing and selling needs. For example, Chapter 11 explains how to develop an action plan to implement your new attack on management prospects.

This program is designed for you to create a replicable and scaleable sales process for yourself and your sales team. Unlike most marketing and sales education programs, Value Forward Selling gives specific strategic, tactical, and communication recommendations and techniques that you can use now to help increase your success selling to management. It doesn't just focus on sales, marketing and strategy techniques—it also focuses on performance changes in your selling behavior to help you reach your sales goals on a replicable basis.

Additionally, different sales and closing techniques are identified for small business sales versus Fortune 1000 sales (i.e., Fortune 1000 technique, Small Business technique).

After you have completed this course, drop me a line about your success.

So, let's get going. Sit back, get comfortable, and let's attack the sales jungle and sell more to management.

Hunt now, or be eaten later!

Regards,

Paul R. DiModica

Overview

Let the selling begin!

Selling to management is a premeditated sport.

Selling to management is based on the survival of:

- the best-trained salespeople

- salespeople who work the hardest

- salespeople who want to win

- salespeople who know how to communicate value to management that stimulates action steps to buy

- salespeople who force prospects to prove they are qualified buyers

- salespeople who engage management with the value of their products or services

- marketing executives who work in tandem with the sales team to help sell

- marketing staff who implement techniques to create qualified, inbound sales leads for the sales team

This book will teach you how to communicate value up front, find clients, present like a pro, and close deals, but it can't teach you the desire to succeed. If you can't pick up the phone and cold call, network with pizzazz, handle proposal objections from a tough chief executive officer, or the drilling and probing of a small business owner because you are afraid, then you should get out of professional sales.

Selling to management is a contact sport. You must train and be prepared for the big game.

Selling is a profession.

Selling to management successfully takes confidence.

Business peers sell more than vendors!

Chapter 1

Understanding Management Prospects

After reading this chapter, you will know:

- Who you are and why management should buy from you

- Why you should focus all of your energies on selling to management only

- Who is considered to be management

- Why selling to management shortens your sales cycle

- The misperceptions of professional selling

- Why most salespeople do not sell to management

Who Are You and Why Should Management Buy From You?

Simple questions. The usual answer is *we're the best at what we do,* or *we have the best product,* but if everyone says the same thing, why should a prospect believe you over the next salesperson?

Your answer is what sets you apart from your competition and intrigues a management prospect enough to take your call. By the end of this book, you'll be able to answer these questions and understand what really sets you apart from your competition.

Why You Should Focus All of Your Energies on Selling to Management Only

Today, more than ever, the goal of all salespeople is to increase the efficiency in selling their products or services. As a salesperson, you must continually deal with prospects who are too busy to respond to the increasing number of sales contacts they are exposed to on a daily basis. The fact that a prospect doesn't want to talk with you is not a personal attack. It is just a response to salespeople in general. Yet, as a professional salesperson, it is your job to penetrate a prospect's "no-talk zone," communicate the value of your product and service, negotiate pricing, and collect sales revenue for your firm.

So, you have two choices. You can either talk to anyone in the targeted company who will listen to you, or deal with the decision maker and bypass all of the bureaucracy that supervisors force you to go through.

It's your choice.

By focusing all of your energy on selling to management, you will improve your sales closing ratio dramatically, increase your compensation, and spend less time working with unqualified prospects.

If this is true, then why doesn't everybody do this?

To be successful with management, you must earn the right to sell them. It is not an automatic right . . . *it is an earned right*. In fact, most sales training methods fail because of this very reason. They over-complicate the sales process by pushing you to the middle of the prospect's organizational chart and into the *slow as you go* sales cycle dominated by supervisors who are simply professional lookers—a process that can result in sales cycles lasting two years or longer.

Of course, the problem with this is most salespeople don't have two-year sales quotas. Either you reach or get near your quota this year . . . or you will be looking for a new job next year.

Most current sales methods that discuss selling to management as a goal use marketing and sales techniques that drive you away from management and into the arms of supervisors who just waste your time.

Then, through a slow and tedious process, these sales methods teach you to manage complex variables and egos of all of the supervisor contacts you now have to deal with as you slowly try to climb back up the organizational chart to management, the level you should have started with in the first place.

What a waste of time.

If you want to sell more, sell to management only.

Don't trust a supervisor to be a better salesperson than you are.

Selling is hard enough, even for full-time professionals. Every time you launch your sales cycle by talking to supervisors about your product or service, you are risking your sales commission. When selling to supervisors, subliminally you are saying *take all of the information that I give, filter it, edit it, and then pass it on to your boss when you think it's appropriate.*

In essence, all of the training and experience you have as a professional salesperson evaporates as soon as you make your product or service presentation to the supervisor . . . and there goes your commission—because they are not you! They are accountants, buyers, directors, or department managers. Regardless of their job function, they are not trained salespeople. So when they describe the value of your product or service to their boss, they will never be as effective as you or manage the questions the boss asks like you would.

The goal of Value Forward Selling is to use a sales process where you communicate your value before you talk to the prospect which allows them to see the value of your business offering. This process is accomplished throughout the sales cycle to eliminate competition, shorten your sales cycle, and validate to the prospect that you are a *business peer*.

Most companies pull their value behind them by talking about how great their product or service is. Then they end up being pushed back by qualified prospects because the prospect does not believe them. It's not that prospects don't believe you personally; instead it's a defensive reaction because most prospects don't believe any salesperson on the first introduction.

A *value forward* model of sales continually communicates your business value up front, so the management prospect can identify your value before you start trying to sell to them.

Who Is Considered To Be Management?

It depends on what kind of product or service you sell and the price point of your sale. If you are selling $10 million jets to Fortune 1000 firms, then the senior executive you may be targeting could be the Chief Financial Officer (CFO). Conversely, if you are selling consulting or professional services to the small business market where annual revenues are under $10 million, you should be calling on the Chief Executive Officer (CEO). Likewise, if you are selling software to automate the human resource department, then you should be targeting the Vice President of Human Resources (HR). When you are selling below the title of director, you are usually already in a commodity position.

The rule of thumb is to never call below the title of a director. (In this book, "management" generally means directors and above.) Follow this rule and you will sell more.

Why Selling to Management Shortens Your Sales Cycle

Let's be honest. Most sales methods pull you down into the middle of the prospect's organizational chart. Then, your sales process becomes a tedious, slow climb up the organization chart to the person you should have contacted first.

This process is complex and requires tremendous account management to make progress. Do these middle organizational chart sales methods work? Sure, but who wants to spend a disproportionate amount of time talking to supervisors? **Supervisors are professional lookers.** They waste your time, don't tell the truth, and disrupt the time management of your sales cycle and sales quota. Even in complicated sales involving multiple decision contacts or corporate divisions, you should always start your sales cycle with management. **Why?** Because senior executives never waste their time, so they will not waste your time.

Management personnel are more knowledgeable and direct in their communications and will not waste time. They tell the truth more often to salespeople.

Price is important to supervisors, not management. Supervisors focus on features, functions, and price. Senior executives focus on their impression of how your product or service can help their business (or department) increase profits, decrease costs, or manage consequences. **Any time you sell to supervisors, you automatically position yourself as a commodity.** Supervisors often compare the pricing of your product or service to their own annual compensation or to what they can personally afford. If your offering doesn't meet their perceptions of what it's worth, they dismiss it as too expensive.

Management wants to know who you have worked with, because they base their decisions on your association with their peers.

Management knows it is not that important in the beginning of a sales cycle to focus only on brand. They would buy from the XYZ Company if that salesperson could prove value.

Management is more concerned with how your product or service will help them run their business better—not how many times you take them to dinner. "Relationship selling" is a concept whereby salespeople extend their sales cycle, convince themselves and their management team they are making progress, and stuff prospect activity into their sales forecasts to look busy. It is not a process for management to buy.

Selling to management is the fastest, most direct way of closing more product or service deals.

- ▶ It's direct

- ▶ It's focused

- ▶ It's to the point

- ▶ It's based on value and business improvement

Five Fallacies of Professional Selling

As a professional salesperson, regardless of whether you are selling a product or a service, there are five universal fallacies that you must deal with on a daily basis. They are:

1. Prospects always tell the truth.

2. Price is the most important buying criterion.

3. Prospects check references.

4. Prospects always buy brand.

5. Relationships matter before the first sale.

All of these are assumptions and false beliefs. Let's look at each one in more detail.

Fallacy Number 1: Prospects always tell the truth. If you have any sales experience, you know this is not true. How many times has a prospect told you:

- Your product or service was exactly what he or she wanted and no other competitor was in the running.

- They were going to make the decision during the next two weeks.

- You had the order.

- You got the deal and they would send you a purchase order during the next week.

The fact is, prospects do not always tell the truth. They may not lie directly, but they mislead, misinform, and cause professional salespeople to incorrectly forecast their sales activity to the management team over and over.

Fallacy Number 2: Price is the most important buying criterion. Study after study shows that price is not the most important buying criterion, however, most buyers today are savvy negotiators when it comes to price.[1] Their job as a buyer is to get the lowest price. Your job as a professional salesperson is to get the highest price.

Many buyers (both management and others) have read books on negotiation and attended negotiation seminars or workshops. In fact, most buyers **are better trained** than salespeople on how to negotiate.

▶ Most buyers know to ask for the lowest price first, and then work from there.

▶ Most buyers know if they give verbal orders, the salesperson will commit to his/her sales forecast or management team he/she got the

---

[1] Studies referenced in this publication include surveys from BDM News, HighTechCEO, and DigitalHatch, as well as information obtained through third-party research aggregators.

deal. Then the buyer starts asking for price concessions or talking about competitors.

▶ Most buyers know they should start negotiating at the end of the month or end of the quarter to put pressure on the salesperson to make his/her forecasted sales quota (or target).

Yet, in spite of all these negotiation tactics, price is still not the most important buying criterion.

Value is the most important criterion—not pricing.

Fallacy Number 3: Prospects check references. Most prospects do not check references. If you give them ten, they may call two. Prospects assume that your references must be happy or you wouldn't have provided them.

Fallacy Number 4: Prospects always buy brand. Although many marketing people love to talk about building brand, and brand selling is great for the business-to-consumer market; in the business-to-business market, using your firm's branding can get in the way of selling when you are selling to management. Why? Because every brand has both good and bad perceptions attached to it based on the receiver's understanding at the time it is heard.

It doesn't matter if what they heard about your brand is true. From the receiver's point of view, it *is* true. They may have read something in a trade publication or a national newspaper about your firm or they may have had a business acquaintance describe your product or service incorrectly.

Or worse, your firm is so big that your brand has become generic and does not exactly describe how your product or service creates value for the prospect, so they immediately dismiss you. This happens all the time. For example:

- You work for a large pharmaceutical company known for one popular drug

- Prospects think your company only sells customer relationship management software

- You sell loose diamonds and your prospects don't know you sell completed jewelry

In each of these examples, your firm's brand got in the way of selling. Prospects either don't return your phone calls or they ignore you because they have made judgments about what you want to sell them.

Fallacy Number 5: Relationships matter *before* the first sale. Salespeople have been taught they must make the prospect like them or have a *relationship* with the prospect before the prospect will buy. The fact of the matter is relationships with prospects start *after* they make a purchase. People who talk about relationship sales methods are really talking about a long sales cycle with a prospect who may or may not be a qualified buyer and then holding on until (hopefully) they wear them down to buy.

The fact is, *you do not have a relationship with a prospect until after the second sale.* Before the first sale (during the pre-sales cycle), you interact with prospects who feed you inaccurate data about potential sales. After the first sale (the post-sales cycle), you no longer have to prove the value you said you could deliver. Having lunch, going to a ball game, or chatting on the phone with a prospect is not a relationship. Somehow, professional salespeople have come to believe that to sell more, they must entertain more, talk more, or meet more people at the prospect's firm.

This is always wrong.

Here are some common situations many salespeople experience:

- ▶ You have a great relationship with a prospect, they always take your calls and meet with you when you stop in . . . but they bought from your competitor.

- ▶ You keep meeting with a prospect . . . but they never buy.

▶ You get on the "short list" of vendors, but you lose the deal after spending more than six months meeting with every key contact in the company that would talk with you.

▶ You lose a deal to a competitor you have never heard of, nor did the prospect mention them as being a potential vendor.

Have any of these situations ever happened to you? Realize prospects buy based on your ability to fix their business pain, not how many times you bought them lunch.

Yes, having a positive working interaction with prospects is important. But helping them fix their business pain means more. Prospects, especially management, want to respect you as a business peer— as someone who can help them do their jobs better, not someone to invite to their daughter's wedding.

Why Most Salespeople Do Not Sell to Management More Often

Selling to management takes specific sales techniques, premeditated actions, and knowledge of how to communicate like a business peer. Many times, based on the environment they operate in, salespeople take the path of least resistance when trying to sell. It's always easier to sell to supervisors, but it is a longer sales cycle. Remember, supervisors are professional lookers. Many times they are waiting for your call. Have you ever noticed that supervisors often schedule vendor meetings at 11:00 a.m. so you can take them to lunch?

When a sales manager tells a salesperson to penetrate a key account and the salesperson fails to get through to the senior executive that is making the decisions, most salespeople take the path of least resistance and call on a supervisor, to appear as if they are making progress with the prospect. But—selling to supervisors just slows up your sales cycle.

Selling to Management is a Premeditated Sport

Selling to management requires a planned premeditated approach, not a shoot-from-the-hip-and-make-it-up-as-you-go sales approach.

Value Forward Selling is a process of using correct communication, precise action steps, and tactical sales methods to induce management to buy from you. **It requires hard work on your part.**

Remember, you must earn the right to sell to management. You do not automatically have the right just because you are a salesperson.

Also, selling to management shortens sales cycles because management will not deal with you if you waste their time or don't know what you are doing. **Management does not have patience for unprepared salespeople. Supervisors do.**

Review and Exercises

1. If a prospect were to ask why they should buy from you, what would your typical answer be? Write it down. If that response vaguely resembles *we are the best*, then take it a step further and write down specific points about what makes you the best and your product or service better than your competitors' (e.g. number of years in business, list of repeat clients, reliability of product, quality of materials, etc.). Now reword your response so you can communicate why they should buy from you. Practice this response until it becomes automatic.

2. When someone asks *what do you sell*, how would you reply? Write down your answer. The typical response is a product or service, e.g., *I sell pharmaceuticals, I sell software, I sell airplanes.* Now reword your answer so that it communicates *how* your product or service increases revenue, decreases expenses, or manages risks. For example, *I sell the ability to reduce manufacturing costs.* Next, write down anticipated questions to your new communication, e.g., *How do you do that? What does that entail?* Lastly, write down your responses to these questions and practice them. Also, be prepared for any unexpected questions.

Chapter 1
Understanding Management Prospects

Chapter 2

Developing Your Sales Value Proposition

After reading this chapter, you will know:

- How to position yourself as a business peer

- What is a sales value proposition

- Why you need a sales value proposition

- How to become a pain management specialist and sell more

- How to develop your sales value proposition

How to Position Yourself as a Business Peer

When selling to management, perception is reality.

To maximize your success, communicate who you and your company are and why the senior executive should talk to you.

As I mentioned earlier, most companies pull their value behind them when trying to sell to management by telling how great their products or services are. These marketing methods usually get little traction because all vendors say their products or services are great and prospects just don't believe anyone on the first pass.

To improve your management prospect penetration success, you need to develop a *value forward* statement, not some nebulous, market-driven blurb that paints a vague picture of who you are. It should be a direct, calculated statement that tells the receiver how you are different and how you can help the senior executive increase income, decrease expenses, or manage risks.

This is not to be confused with *branding*. *Branding* does not generate revenue. Remember:

▶ Advertising is not revenue

▶ PR is not revenue

▶ Marketing is not revenue

▶ Sales *is* revenue

When you create a sales value proposition, you must develop an outbound integrated sales, marketing, and strategy phrase (or hook) so prospects see you as a peer, not as a vendor. When setting up this approach,

there are three basic questions that must be answered.
They are:

1. Why will management buy from you?

2. Why will management *not* buy from you?

3. What "visual value" does your product or
   service deliver to management?

Although these appear to be simple questions, the
answers are, in fact, complex and layered, like an onion
that must be peeled back. These questions must be
closely examined to understand how they affect your
ability to sell.

When salespeople consider these questions, they
usually jump to conclusions and assume that if their
firm is small or if they are selling against more
financially stable competitors, they are at an immediate
disadvantage because they lack positioning and
advertising funding. **This is a misperception.**

When selling to management, company positioning is
developed on a contact-by-contact basis as a result of
the sales techniques, marketing methods, and
communication style you use to connect and interact
with the executive prospect.

Often, corporate branding messages used by large
companies get in the way of selling and can be

detrimental to salespeople trying to sell to
management. We hear quite a bit about company
branding and the correct way to position your firm,
but the true process for an account manager to sell to
management in volume is to develop a unique sales
value proposition that is **targeted to the needs of the
buyer.**

Trying to sell to a Fortune 1000 or a small business
owner requires getting your company's message
through the volume of inbound salespeople that senior
executives in small and large companies are exposed to
every day. Traditional sales training recommends
selling features and benefits, such as selling the size of
the steak, not the steak itself. However, you will not
get very far unless you reach the decision maker.

Even worse, many sales training methods talk about
dealing with supervisors because of their influence in
the sales process. Yes, you must deal with supervisors,
but they should never be an entry point in your sales
cycle.

Don't just be *Smith Jewelry Wholesaler, Paul's Web and
Graphic Design Firm, Hillman Consulting;* or describe
yourself by saying, *We market jet engines to airline
companies.* Instead, think more strategically when talking
to management. **Position yourself differently.**

Get through the noise. The way to do this is by
creating a unique visual picture of who you are and

how you are different, while simultaneously communicating how you can help your prospect. We call this management-selling tool a "visual brochure". A visual brochure is a picture you paint in the mind of the buyer based on the words you say and the words you don't say. Through the delivery of your verbal presentation, proposal formats, and marketing messages with management, you are creating visual brochures that communicate either vendor or peer status to the prospect.

Based on what they hear and see from you and what they don't hear or see, management makes quick judgments to either let you continue interacting with them or reject you as someone who does not bring value to the table. Once they reject your status as a peer and see you as a vendor, they either dismiss you outright or send you (or have their secretary send you) to a supervisor. Conversely, if you meet or communicate using this method with supervisors, they will generally invite you to start your sales cycle with them and waste your (and their) time just to look busy to their bosses. Supervisors do not need a peer-to-peer relationship; they only want a vendor relationship—no matter what they tell you.

One strategic mistake many sales executives make when interacting with management for the first time is explaining to the prospect why their firm, product, or service is "great." **Being a salesperson does not give**

you the right to sell to management. You have to earn this right. Sometimes salespeople have a tendency to project their needs onto the prospect; they assume management should listen.

As a salesperson, you project your needs to feel good about what you sell, to hit your sales quota, to increase your commission, and to keep your job. These personal issues are what prevent you from communicating the real reason the prospect should buy from you. The fact is management doesn't care about you. Prospects only care about how you are going to help them be more successful in their job.

By creating a visual brochure for the prospect that paints a picture of how your product or service can add value to their business and how you will help them become more successful, you can reduce the barriers they automatically put up, thereby allowing you the opportunity to sell them more. So, the first step of creating a management visual brochure is to develop a sales value proposition for your firm, product, and/or service.

What Is a Sales Value Proposition (SVP)?

A *sales value proposition* (SVP) is the hook that makes you unique to get past the management filter of being seen ONLY as a salesperson. SVPs are some of the business tools in the Value Forward tool box. They are used in all communications with your prospects, both directly through personal interaction and indirectly through your marketing materials.

When developing your SVP, it should appeal to the executive and the industry you are trying to reach. If you are calling on the president of a 100-person company or the CFO of a Fortune 500 firm, you need to think like they do. Ask yourself, *what are the business problems they are facing on a daily basis; what business pain does my product or service fix?*

Management never buys jet engines, software, consulting, pharmaceutical inventory, or wholesale jewelry without first knowing exactly what business pain the jet engine, software, pharmaceutical inventory, or wholesale jewelry will fix.

Why Do You Need a Sales Value Proposition?

For you to sell to management, you must stop thinking like a salesperson and start thinking like a strategist who is a **pain management specialist**.

Management buying decisions are centered around three elements:

1. How to increase income

2. How to decrease expenses

3. How to manage their business risks

That's it. So when developing your sales value proposition and thinking about how to position your firm to sell to management, you must first "think through" **how your product or service fixes your prospect's business pain by increasing income, decreasing expenses, or managing their business risks**.

How to Become a Pain Management Specialist and Sell More

Today, more than ever, trying to sell your product or service based on its features will not work when trying to sell to management. Management buys a product or service based on its ability to fix their business pain. **It's as simple as that.**

What pain does a business executive have?

Business pain for executives centers around their ability to increase income, decrease expenses, or manage risks on a daily basis. For example:

▶ You are not selling wholesale tubing to the VP of Operations. You are selling the ability to reduce manufacturing costs.

▶ You are not selling loose diamonds to the president of a jewelry wholesaler. You are selling increased inventory turns that will increase top line revenue.

▶ You are not selling IT accounting software. You are selling a tool that helps the CFO increase his cash collection through faster vendor billing.

To sell to management, you must stop talking about features, functions, and attributes and start talking about what is important to them. **You do not sell products or services, but the result your product or service delivers and the ability to have a positive financial effect (directly or indirectly) on the prospect's business. Your product or service is a business tool to drive management results.** For example:

- **You don't sell payroll outsourcing**—you sell a service that reduces labor (reduces expenses)

- **You don't sell pharmaceuticals**—you sell a product that has a greater gross margin (increases income)

- **You don't sell software**—you sell a product that reduces paperwork and labor (reduces expenses)

- **You don't sell consulting**—you sell a service that increases employee productivity (increases income)

- **You don't sell advice**—you sell protection from IRS audits (consequence management)

How do you discover the business pains your management prospects must deal with on a daily basis?

▶ Read industry specific magazines that management prospects are likely to read. For Fortune 1000 companies, subscribe to *CFO*, *CIO*, *CIO Insight*, *Fortune*, *Forbes*, *Business Week*, *Inc.*, and *The Wall Street Journal*. For smaller companies, search articles in magazines like *Inc.*, *FSB Fortune Small Business*, and *Entrepreneur*. Also, look in trade publications for the industry you are selling to, such as *Nation's Restaurant News* if you are selling restaurant equipment or *Bio IT World* if you sell healthcare products.

▶ Visit five to ten of your prospects' web sites and look for the areas they are focusing on. Document the same business words all of your prospects have on their web sites used to describe their companies. If your prospects are using specific industry words, then these words are important to them and their industry.

▶ Read the "Press Release" section of their web sites and read any quotes their vice presidents and top executives are giving to the public. Usually these quotes contain information on what business issues (pain) they are trying to manage.

▶ If you are selling to public companies, read their annual and quarterly reports, specifically the "Letter to the Stockholder" section from the CEO. Usually the CEO discusses the company's financial success or failure and provides reasons for that success or failure. In this section you may find the business pains they are trying to fix (or have fixed). Additionally, look at trade web sites in their industry to see which subject matter is being repeated.

How to Develop Your Sales Value Proposition

When building your sales value proposition, plan your approach by following these seven steps:

Step 1.   Study your competition. It is *not* what you sell. It is *who* you sell against.

Step 2.   Research your targeted customers' needs. What is their pain? What are the words and vernacular of their industry? What words do they use in industry trade publications? What business pains do they talk about on industry trade association web sites?

Step 3. Develop a new concept or industry term. Be creative and use industry terms based on your customers' vernacular.

Step 4. Write a white paper on your new concept. Push to get it published in trade publications.

Step 5. Develop a presentation and marketing collateral to match your new concept. For example, your presentation might be a slide show, whiteboard, or demo and your collateral might include the white paper or brochures.

Step 6. Develop a telemarketing script to match your new concept. This is what intrigues the prospect enough to take your call.

Step 7. Create an in-person sales presentation that matches your sales value proposition concept. This is the last element that ties your sales value proposition to all of your sales tools.

After studying the web sites of your competition, your prospects, and the industry you are targeting, **you should develop your sales value proposition as follows**:

1. Use five to seven words to build your sales value proposition. It should be short, direct, and succinct in order to instantly intrigue the listener.

2. Use the word *specialist*. Management buys from specialists, not generalists. Never use the word *expert*. The word *expert* implies a legal verification that you may need to validate later.

3. Use a vertical word from the industry you are selling into (e.g., manufacturing, pharmaceutical, wholesalers, IT, distributors, etc.).

4. Inside your sales value proposition, use words that imply how your product or service increases income, decreases expenses, or manages risks.

5. Identify the business consequences if management does not buy a product or service like yours (or your competitors') that increases income, decreases expenses, or manages risks. This is called *consequence management*.

Also, when developing your sales value proposition, paint a broad picture to make it harder for the prospect to know exactly what you are talking about without precise clarification from you. The goal is to **intrigue them enough to see you as a business strategist** who can help fix their business pain. Remember, you are not selling a product or service, but the *financial results* your product or service creates (directly or indirectly) for management.

If your firm specializes in selling products or services to a specific vertical, try to use that industry name in your sales value proposition (e.g., Specialists in Casino Player Retention). If your firm sells products or services to a broad market, be more generic in your sales value proposition (e.g., Recurring Revenue Stream Management Specialists).

Below are additional examples of sales value propositions that I developed for clients whom I consulted with. All of them have worked.

- Specialists in Asset Enlargement for Financial Service Firms

- Specialists in Inventory Personalization Controls for the Retail Industry

- Migration Management Specialists for the **X** Industry

- Transaction Business Specialists for the **X** Industry

- Profit Improvement Specialists for the **X** Industry

- Guest Retention Management Specialists for Hotels

- Web Connectivity Management Specialists

- Retention Management Specialists for the **X** Industry

Always look for a term that is not currently used in your industry, but addresses a benefit that is important to your industry. If needed, you can borrow terms from other industries.

Test your SVPs. Once you have developed several suggestions, insert them in a major Internet search engine to see what comes up. If your SVP is used by another industry and might confuse your prospect with what you do, choose another one.

Just be different! Remember, management sees you as you see yourself.

▶ If you are a jewelry major account salesperson, become a Retail Inventory Expense Control Specialist.

▶ If you are a wholesaler, become a Wholesale Inventory Turn Management Specialist.

▶ If you are an IT salesperson selling software to the hospitality market, become a Hospitality Customer Profit Improvement Specialist.

▶ If you sell bicycle add-on accessories to manufacturers, become a Bicycle Margin Improvement Specialist.

When prospects *see* your visual brochure, they will not see you *as just a salesperson* but instead as a business strategist who can help fix their business pain of how to increase income, decrease expenses, or manage risks.

Once this vision is clear, you are now a business peer instead of a salesperson. Your business barriers are reduced and your sales cycle can move forward.

Case Study—Developing Your SVP: A Hotel Product

Several years ago, I accepted a position as VP of Sales and Marketing for a hotel product company with annual revenues of about $20 million. Our average sale ranged from $400,000 to over $1 million and included all of the ongoing services. Our market was worldwide and we had many competitors entering every year.

When I was hired, I was told we would be deploying our updated product during the next six months. As it often happens in privately funded companies, our product development slowed.

Instead of having the updated product in six months, the delivery date had slipped to eighteen months.

So what could I do? The CEO said no new money was available for development. My sales account managers were complaining they were losing deals to competitors, and the Board of Directors kept asking me, *Where's your sales revenue?*

Does this sound familiar?

Here is what I reasoned. Since our product was a mature product and our competitors' products were newer, we held the upper hand in selling our proven status to help hotels lower costs. The key at that point was to position our sales value proposition around our strengths and our competitors' weaknesses. Here are the steps I took to achieve this:

Step 1.   After doing some research on our competitors' products, I discovered their products (both older versions and newer ones) were weak in customer service in the hotel area and our product excelled.

Step 2.   Doing additional research on my prospects, I discovered that guest management is always a big issue for hotels and was a major talking point for hotel management. Knowing this, I developed a complete sales value proposition based on this one area.

Step 3.   I created a new industry term called *Guest Retention Management*.

Step 4.   I wrote a white paper on the concept and got it published in several trade publications.

Step 5.   I developed custom slide presentations and company brochures to match my marketing.

Step 6.   I developed a verticalized telemarketing script to cold call hotel executives (the GM of single locations, the VP of Operations of chains, etc.) about our unique services.

Step 7.   I created a specialized sales presentation on how we were *Guest Retention Specialists*.

With our new sales value proposition in place, my sales team and I attacked the market, and consistently increased sales quarter after quarter. Since this was in the early '90s, CRM systems were not even invented yet, so our *Guest Retention Management* system for hotels became a hit.

As you can see, I was a **Hunter**. Instead of caving into sales and management pressure, I developed a unique sales value proposition to beat my competitors.

I was different.

I made up a new sales value proposition that the executives were curious to hear about and my competitors couldn't compete against. How could they—I made it up! I was different and it worked. In this case, I created the market perception and made it become a reality.

In sales to management, perception is reality.

Case Study—Developing Your SVP: Professional and Internet Services

While working with another company, I was asked to help launch a new division that sold business development consulting, web development, project work, and managed services.

Knowing that this market space was overwhelmed with tens of thousands of competitors in the United States, I knew I would have to develop a unique sales value proposition to compete and succeed.

Using the seven steps of the sales value proposition program I had developed, I implemented another new marketing campaign, as follows:

Step 1.   I researched my competitors and discovered they were focused on selling singular services, one at a time, usually to the company Chief Information Officer, or CIO.

Step 2.   I researched my prospects and discovered the CEOs of these venture capital (VC) funded startups were spending a disproportionate amount of their business time raising venture capital funding and

---

managing their investors' expectations. These expectations, usually written into the contracts CEOs sign when they receive funding from VCs, are known as *milestones* and *ratchets*.

Step 3. I created a new industry term called *milestone management*.

Step 4. I wrote a white paper on this concept and had it published.

Step 5. I developed a custom slide presentation, marketing collateral, and web site to complement our new sales value proposition, *Milestone Management Specialists*.

Step 6. I developed a verticalized telemarketing script to cold call CEOs to discuss our milestone management services.

Step 7. I created a specialized, in-person sales presentation to communicate our milestone management program. I also developed sales value proposition talking points that highlighted my services' ability to increase revenue, reduce expenses and manage risks.

So, what happened? My business development managers and I began cold calling CEOs of VC-funded companies, scheduled in-person meetings, and closed 50% of those deals on the first contact. Yes, that's correct—**50%!** Once we got in front of the CEOs as *Milestone Management Specialists*, we talked about "helping them increase their valuation and funding opportunities by supplying them services that would help them meet their milestones on time and under budget."

Of course, these services were web development, product development, staffing, and business consulting which were identical to all of our competitors' offerings and perceived by many prospects to be commodity services. We were successful because we attacked the pain of CEOs from a top-down approach—selling our services to meet their needs (which were the milestone and ratchet clauses in their VC contracts). Concurrently, we were bypassing our competitors who were calling on the CIOs, HR managers, and IT managers.

By using this sales value proposition method, we were able to beat out well-established Fortune 500 services and small private companies because their major account sales forces were focused on communicating generic-sounding company-positioning statements.

We sounded different. We acted different. And we got the business.

You are probably starting to notice a pattern. The key is to be different from everyone else. If you are like me, you always seem to be meeting larger and more established competitors. If you push against your competitors, you will lose. Instead, use stealth, like a Navy Seal. Evaluate your competition and prospects, determine what weapons you will use, and, under the cover of night, attack and conquer.

Be unique. Develop a new market position, package it, and then communicate your story to the world and key decision makers.

By using the right words, you can paint your picture!

Once you have created your sales value proposition, you can then develop talking points on how the benefits of your product or service can increase income, decrease expenses or manage risks.

If you are selling to a senior executive or the president of a small company, the decisions made by that executive are almost always centered on these three issues—**revenue, expenses and risks.** These are the three elements every senior executive wants to hear. Tie these benefits to your SVP presentation and you will get a positive response. Talk about your product or service without addressing these areas and you will fail.

In fact, if you sell products or services to multiple verticals, you should develop unique sales value propositions and telemarketing scripts for each vertical.

Your sales value proposition needs to be different, so *be creative*!

Studies over the past several years revealed that the majority of management gathered their information and business process data *from vendors*—that's people like you and I.[2] The research behind this information indicated that most executives are just too busy to read all of the trade publications in their market. So they rely on vendors to keep them up to date.

This indicates executives are always looking for the newest business process to make them successful. As a professional salesperson, this means when you call on them with your sales value proposition, they will want to know more if they have never heard of your unique offering or how you can help them fix their business issues.

At times, the selling proposition you create may be different from your company's generic value

---

[2] Studies referenced in this publication include surveys from BDM News, HighTechCEO, and DigitalHatch, as well as information obtained through third-party research aggregators.

proposition. I have used this approach with *every* firm I have ever worked for.

It always works. *Never be a generalist, always be a specialist.*

Earlier in my career, when I was a junior salesperson, I developed my own slide presentations and telemarketing scripts to reinforce my sales value proposition. Later, when I became VP of Sales, I implemented my unique sales value propositions company-wide. Developing your sales value proposition early will help you generate more meetings, make unique presentations, and close a greater percentage of sales.

Being different and using the right words makes key decision makers **LISTEN**.

Review and Exercises

1. Here is a great way to develop your unique sales value proposition. Go to ten of your customers' web sites and print out ten pages from each of them. Then, review the pages and circle any repetitive words they all use in their company copy. Your sales value proposition needs to be generic to a certain degree, but highlighting benefits from the industry to gain the interest of the CEOs you are trying to sell to is critical.

    List those words on a separate sheet of paper and use them to develop your sales value proposition. If your customers are talking about it on their web sites, you can be sure it is important to them. All you need to do is package it for sales consumption.

2. Visit a local bookstore and pick up at least one industry or executive magazine you have never read before. Highlight and remove pages that contain information you want to refer back to and place them in a file so you can reference the information easily.

3. Examine the product or service you are selling. Develop a sales value proposition on that product or service. Follow the seven steps and build your new marketing campaign.

Chapter 2
Developing Your Sales Value Proposition

Chapter 3

Finding Management and Penetrating the No-Talk Zone

After reading this chapter, you will know:

- What parallel imaging is

- How to develop a senior executive dictionary to communicate like a peer

- What words to avoid so you don't sound like a vendor

- What words to use so you sound like a peer

What Is Parallel Imaging?

Parallel imaging is a method of communication whereby you subliminally inform management prospects you are a peer and not a vendor by the words you use and don't use. As discussed before, when you speak to management and gatekeepers, each word and phrase you say paints a visual brochure of who you are and what you are offering. To accomplish parallel imaging, use the language of the buyer to sound like the buyer. When you use the language and terms that executive prospects use, they will see themselves in you and drop the barrier of communication. Later in this chapter, you will learn how to develop an executive dictionary that will be used in parallel imaging.

Senior executives make judgments about salespeople every day. Based on their education; ethnic, social and economic background; gender; geography; and current job position, prospects decide if salespeople are informed, if the product or service can help them succeed in their job, and whether the salesperson has the right to be talking to them. Many times, these decisions are done subconsciously—but they happen nevertheless.

Is it wrong for these people to make judgments? That's a discussion for another book. The point is, if you are trying to sell to management, you must accept that it happens every day.

Once you accept this reality, you can then use parallel imaging techniques to reposition the prospect's biased or incorrect conclusion about you and your company and what value you bring.

Perception is reality when selling to management.

When selling to management, it is important for you to understand the concept of *perception is reality.*

Management bases its buying decisions on impression; not features, function, or price.

Yes, features, function, and price are important to senior executives, but when you get to the boardroom, these issues become less important and are complemented by additional decisions.

Supervisors focus on features, function, and price because they view the business world through a narrow scope. Many times, supervisors subconsciously compare vendor pricing to their annual income to calculate the value of the vendor's price.

- If your product is high-priced compared to the salary of the supervisor, they subliminally judge it negatively.

- If the hourly rate of your service is higher than the supervisor's hourly rate, they subliminally dismiss your offering as too costly.

Selling to supervisors positions you as a commodity. Selling to management allows you to build a perception of *value* on why they should buy from you rather than your competitors. Throughout this program, we are going to give you tools, tactics, and methods to build a *boardroom impression*.

Value is a management word, not a subordinate word. Management always looks at subjective issues on why they should buy from one vendor over another. Although management and supervisors may start at the same level for business requirements, each group determines its buying decisions based on different reasons. Such factors as *psychological ROI* always play into management's decision-making process. (We will discuss psychological ROI in more detail in Chapter 8.) Conversely, using these same sales techniques on supervisors usually never works because their business decisions are always centered on features, function, price, or service deliverables.

Management Entry Point	Non-Management Entry Point
1. Price/business value as presented by salesperson ⬇	1. Price, features, function, service deliverables ⬇
2. How your offering relates to company needs as presented by salesperson ⬇	2. How your offering relates to non-management's personal needs and expectations ⬇
3. Business impression as determined by management ⬇	3. Vendor recommendations to management by non-management ⬇
4. Decision to buy	4. Price value based on non-management's perception ⬇
	5. Business value based on non-management's perception ⬇
	6. How your offering relates to company needs using non-management's input ⬇
	7. Decision to buy

Figure 1. *Comparative Sales Cycle.* The first column shows the sales cycle when you directly communicate with the decision maker. The second column shows the sales cycle when you communicate with a non-decision maker. The gray area emphasizes the steps where you lose control over what is being communicated to the decision maker.

As noted in Figure 1, management's path to making a decision is totally different than non-management's path. Selling to management involves a shorter and more direct sales cycle where you control the communication directly to the decision maker. You are able to move beyond features/function/price elements by creating value for management and turning *perception into reality.*

Since the concept of value is an individually defined attribute, this process gives you flexibility on how you communicate value to each management executive you interact with. Conversely, when you enter the sales cycle with people who are not management executives, **your value is communicated by someone who lacks your communication skills** and many times will subordinate company needs to their personal needs. Additionally, your sales process is elongated and the value of your product or service is exposed to subjective opinion.

Selling to management always gives you the power to increase your sales. Through this *perception is reality* approach, you can build value to warrant higher prices, manage decision influencers, and build barriers of entry for competitors.

How to Develop a Senior Executive Dictionary to Communicate Like a Peer

If you are going to interact with targeted executive prospects and your goal is to communicate a subjective message of value, then you need to bridge the gap that normally exists between the vendor and the prospect through the correct use of language. The quickest way to accomplish this is through the development of what we call a *senior executive dictionary*, a collection of words your targeted prospects use on a daily basis to transact their business functions. These words define their industry specialization and how they see themselves in relation to their peers and business associates.

By emulating their communication vernacular as a vendor, you immediately send subliminal messages you are more like them. Why? Because your normal vendor communication sends a signal to a prospect (or a prospect's administrator) that you are a vendor trying to sell something—specifically, a salesperson about to waste their time. Once this message is received, the prospect throws barriers up in front of the vendor that say *stay away* or even worse *talk to my assistant, just leave me alone*.

But, if you talk like the prospect talks, you send them the message that you are like them, you are a peer, and they should drop some of the barriers of resistance to speak with you.

How do you determine which words to use and which words scare prospects away? Start by collecting words your prospects use. To do this, first you must read the trade publications of the industry you are trying to sell to or the target publications aimed at your prospects by their title. For example, if you are trying to sell the CFO or CIO, you should subscribe to the magazines they read. If you are trying to sell into retail, freight, hospitality, or the healthcare industries, then you should read the respective monthly publications of their professional associations. However, beyond just reading these publications, you need to make note of the unique words and business concepts they discuss.

Organize your senior executive dictionary based on the job titles of the management you want to sell to and the industry verticals you sell into (i.e., CFOs, general managers, vice presidents of human resources, etc.).

Words and Phrases That Make You Sound like a Vendor and Should Be Avoided	Words and Phrases That Make You Sound Like a Peer and Should Be Used
• Sales	• Chat
• Appointment	• Meeting
• Deal	• Firm
• Company	• Engage
• Discuss	• Strategic focus
• Contract	• Scorecard
• Demo	• Tactical use
• Presentation	• Productivity improvement
• Proposal	• Performance improvement
• Invoice	• Executive briefing
• Purchase Order	• Business value
• Pilot or Test Order (or System)	• Return on investment
• Order	• Strategic value
• Technology	• Value-driven
• Software	

Chapter 3
Finding Management and Penetrating the No-Talk Zone

Review and Exercises

1. Develop a senior executive dictionary. Study
    the industry and business magazines your
    prospects read. If you are trying to sell into
    retail, freight, hospitality, or the healthcare
    industries, you should read the monthly
    publications of their respective associations.
    And beyond just reading these publications, you
    need to list the unique words and business
    concepts they discuss. Organize your senior
    executive dictionary based on the titles of the
    management you are selling to and the industry
    verticals you sell into (i.e., CFOs, general
    managers, vice presidents of human resources,
    etc.).

Chapter 3
Finding Management and Penetrating the No-Talk Zone

Chapter 4

Generating Leads: Marketing to Management

After reading this chapter, you will know:

- Why most marketing materials and methods fail to generate qualified leads

- How branding can affect your sales and how to maximize brand effectiveness

- How to maximize lead-generation effectiveness

- The best methods to market and generate sales leads

- Which direct mail programs generate leads

- How to create white papers that can be used as marketing and sales tools

- How to use executive seminars to generate prospects

- What engagement marketing is and how it shortens your sales cycle

- How to use channel partners and networking to build your pipeline

- How to use touch management to communicate with your prospects during an active buying cycle

There are three methods to generate management leads: 1) marketing, 2) networking, and 3) cold calling. As you read this book, you will learn about all three.

Why Most Marketing Materials and Methods Fail to Generate Qualified Management Leads

Marketing to management prospects is different from communicating your product or service attributes to supervisors. Due to the continued onslaught of visual, print, audio, and Internet exposure management receives on a daily basis, they usually discount most marketing messages as *professional spam*. In short, all of those expensive four-color, eight-page brochures are wasted when they are sent to management. **Management does not read brochures.** Why? Because management does not have time to review all the materials they receive on any business day. They are too busy and you end up wasting money. This also applies to electronic CD presentations, online web presentations, and audio CDs.

Do you think a senior vice president of a multi-national company is going to watch your

**interactive CD for fifteen minutes of his/her busy
day?** Nope. At least, it doesn't happen on a consistent
basis. Generating qualified management leads is always
a challenge for professional salespeople and marketing
managers.

On the other hand, supervisors love brochures, CDs,
and web presentation material. It keeps them busy and
fills their need to have an office full of vendor
marketing material. In fact, they will phone you to ask
for more.

**How do you generate management leads if you
are a salesperson seeking to penetrate the
executive boardroom?**

To penetrate the no-talk zone of management, you
need to act like a peer. This peer-to-peer
communication should be supported by all of your
marketing messages (like your sales value proposition)
and must be targeted specifically to the needs and
business pains of the senior executive. Use the
language the targeted executive speaks.

Sending generic marketing materials wastes time,
money, and sometimes burns qualified prospects who
might respond to a peer-to-peer message.

**The goal of marketing is to help the
sales department generate revenue.**

Marketing, in a traditional sense, has always been a staff position (one that costs money), supporting line positions like the sales department (one that generates money). But marketing is moving from a staff position into a line position directly responsible for generating revenue. Through online Internet purchases, direct-mail response purchases, and other methods that generate qualified leads for the sales team, marketing has evolved to become more of a symbiotic contributor to your company's top line revenue goals.

As marketing teams move from a passive staff position to an active line position, they must be held more accountable as well. This new accountability offers additional opportunities and concurrent liabilities to VPs of marketing and marketing managers. As their range of responsibility increases, marketing managers' compensation should be adjusted upward so they are more in line with VPs of sales.

How Branding Can Affect Your Sale

Brand communication programs aggressively used by many marketing departments are tools like any other marketing program. They are designed to generate qualified inbound sales leads and reduce barriers of entry during the sales cycle with targeted prospects.

> ▶ Is brand marketing effective in the business-to-business (B2B) market space?

▶ Does it help or confuse perceptions of your firm, product, or service when prospects recall your brand "top of mind"?

▶ Does brand marketing hamper the success of salespeople?

Let's say you are a vice president at a Fortune 1000 company and I cold called you on the telephone and said, *Hello, this is Paul DiModica. I am calling from the XYZ Company.*

What would be the visual brochure in your mind once you (or your gatekeeper) heard my company name? If I am with a plumbing company, you will think plumbing. If I am with a company known for software, you will think software company.

Many times, brand marketing hampers salespeople's ability to communicate specific business value to targeted management prospects. Why? Because most brand marketing "paints" generic static pictures in the minds of prospects, thus forcing them to quickly draw a conclusion on what the salesperson is calling about, not necessarily what the salesperson is trying to sell.

Brand marketing, when done in broad strokes, actually has a negative effect on the sales cycle by **preventing salespeople from communicating specific**

business value that will resonate with the individual needs of a potential buyer.

Branding works for companies that have one product or one service and when their brand firmly *paints a visual brochure* of what is offered. But most successful firms that start out as a one-product or a one-service company usually try to expand their revenue opportunities with add-on products and services. These new products and services may not be closely related to their core messaging and may ultimately confuse the prospect because the branding has been established. As new line extensions develop, new brand marketing messages must be created to support salespeople for each area.

Is a generic brand good?

Not necessarily. More than ever, prospects are seeking to work with firms that are specialists, not generalists. Communicating broad *big company* images on your company as a whole contradicts clear messaging of why prospects should buy from you. This process of whole-brand marketing encompasses your sales message and suffocates your positioning as a specialist.

When your firm is known for a single product or service, branding limits the range of approaches your salespeople have when prospecting for new sales opportunities and networking with targeted key accounts. Additionally, the effects of brand marketing are not limited to the impact of your direct marketing programs, but also from the demographic background of the receiving prospects. Based on their exposure to your brand by comments from business peers, unproven rumors, and inaccurate press statements, they can again develop preconceived *visual brochures* about what you sell and its value.

Should you deploy broad market brands?

Yes and no. Generic brand marketing that paints your company into a broad market position is not going to help your sales team sell specific products or services that are not recognized by a targeted buyer.

How to Maximize Brand Effectiveness

1. Focus your message on specific lines of products or services rather than generic company messages.

2. Position your branding message on the results your product or service delivers rather than the product or service itself.

3. Communicate how your product or service affects corporate profitability. The most current selection criteria studies on why management buys indicates they focus on purchases that increase income, decrease expenses, or manage

risks. To help your brand drive revenue opportunities, your corporate messaging must be centered on these three variables to communicate your specialized value.

Concurrently, marketing managers who do not drive revenue successfully need to be managed like failing VPs of sales who miss their sales team's quota. When was the last time you heard of a vice president of marketing being fired because the company brochures did not generate leads?

How to Maximize Lead-Generation Effectiveness

Guidelines to Help Manage Marketing Department Lead-Generation Effectiveness

1. Manage the marketing department like the sales department. Give them business metrics that are tied to revenue.

2. Pay vice presidents of marketing on the same scale as vice presidents of sales, hold them responsible on the same level as vice presidents of sales, but terminate them quicker if they do not produce.

3. Pay a commission to your vice president of marketing or marketing manager based on the vice president of sales' quota.

4. Have the marketing department focus the largest percentage of its annual budget on generating qualified sales leads.

Remember...

Marketing is not revenue.

Advertising is not revenue.

PR is not revenue.

Branding is not revenue.

Revenue is revenue.

The Best Methods to Generate Management Sales Leads

The top methods of reaching management prospects are:

1. Direct mail

2. White papers

3. Executive seminars

4. Engagement marketing

5. Channel partners

6. Networking

7. Cold calling

Each one of these marketing and sales processes can stand alone, but when integrated as a complete program, they generate a continuous flow of qualified management leads that will keep a salesperson or an entire team busy.

Normally, when salespeople (or marketing departments) see this list, they pick the one method they like the best and ignore the rest. This is a subjective performance issue based on their level of comfort. Doing this will limit your sales success. Using all of these methods to some degree, as an integrated approach, will increase your inbound qualified sales lead opportunities. When combined with cold calling, your lead generation will prosper.

This chapter will discuss methods 1 through 6. Chapter 5 will is dedicated to cold calling because that is the most effective way to quickly build your pipeline.

Which Direct Mail Programs Generate Leads

Traditional Direct Mail: Letters and Response Cards

Sending traditional direct mail to the management of a Fortune 1000 company and presidents of small firms is usually a waste of time and money. On a daily basis they are inundated with junk mail from other business-to-business companies trying to sell them on some new opportunity. (Think about how much junk mail *you* receive.) Usually, management has executive assistants sift through their mail and they will not even see it. If your marketing department wants to spend its budget on a direct mail program to convince your management team they are busy, that's fine. But proportionately, the percentage of interest will be small.

CB CB CB

Q: **How do you get management to respond to direct mail?**

A: The key is to focus on your sales value proposition to get their attention based on their business pain and **specific marketing devices that make you look like a peer, not a vendor.**

CB CB CB

The Book Method

One successful direct mail alternative is to send management a business book with an inscription inside discussing your sales value proposition and requesting to chat with them about your sales value proposition. The book needs to be the most current release (hopefully they have not read it yet) on business strategies and it should somehow tie into your unique sales value proposition.

ೞ   ೞ   ೞ

Q: **Why a book?**

A: Because:

> Books are a lot more expensive than a direct sales letter, so the senior executive will not receive very many.

> It will arrive in a box, so it will be hard to miss.

> It will open the door for your call requesting a meeting (*I am the person who sent the book*).

> It will confirm that the senior executive actually read your inscription.

Assistants always remember the person who sent a book. Just tell them, *I'm the person who sent the book*, and they may pass you right to the executive. If they say it looks like a great book (and you get to speak to the executive) send a copy to the assistant (or hand-deliver a copy to her when you meet her boss).

CB CB CB

Q: **Does it work?**

A: Yes. Let's take a look at the case study below as an example.

Case Study—Generating Leads: The Book Method

Several years ago, I was working with a client who wanted to reach the vice president of operations of Fortune 1000 clients quickly.

To launch the program, I created their sales value proposition, developed supporting marketing materials to match the sales value proposition message and the business pain message, and then mailed out one hundred books, each in a separate box to the senior executives.

The boxes were shipped three-day delivery and on the fifth day, we followed up with a phone call. Within one week, we had seven meetings (7%) with vice presidents of operations. Within thirty days, we had sixteen meetings (16%), and three of these sixteen *called us* to schedule directly.

Did it work? Yes.

ભ ભ ભ

Q: **Will the book program work with small companies with employee base ranges from ten to one hundred?**

A: Definitely. Small company CEOs and management executives receive even less attention than Fortune 1000 executives. Getting a free $20 book from you will generate discussion and should open the door for a meeting.

ભ ભ ભ

Q: **Is it expensive?**

A: No, because if you have developed the right sales value proposition, are targeting the right prospect, and communicating a compelling story, that $20 investment could be worth thousands of dollars in business.

ભ ભ ભ

When marketing to management, sending your company brochure immediately positions you as a vendor. Supervisors read company brochures, management does not. Management is simply too busy to read a four-color corporate piece that talks about how great your product or service is. Instead, most corporate brochures sent to management are placed in a special file that is emptied every day. Additionally, most brochures are developed based on the *mud theory*, i.e., a corporate brochure is filled with a little bit about everything. Essentially, most brochures do not stimulate a senior executive to contact you.

Have you ever seen a senior executive on a long airplane trip reading vendor brochures? Of course not! What they will bring is a business book.

To act like a business peer, the next time you are trying to penetrate the no-talk zone of management, send them a business book and then follow-up with a phone call three days after they receive the book.

Sending a book is a business peer-to-peer method of interaction. It's almost like two senior executives sitting in a boardroom talking about a great book they read over the weekend.

On the inside of the book inscribe:

> *Dear Mr./Ms. Prospect,*
>
> *I saw this book and thought it was intriguing, so I decided to send it to you. My firm works with [INSERT THEIR TITLE] like yourself because we are specialists in [INSERT YOUR SALES VALUE PROPOSITION].*

If possible, I would like to chat for twenty minutes about our different programs and services. Enjoy the book.

Regards,
[YOUR NAME]

Book Mailing Guidelines

1. Select a book that is newer than thirty days and is currently on a business best-seller list.

2. Read the book first to make sure there are no politically incorrect comments.

3. Always send the book via three-day delivery or U.S. Priority Mail.

4. Send books on business strategy, success, or management methods. Never send a book on a specific industry subject matter, like manufacturing, technology or jewelry wholesaling.

Why does the book method work?

Business books have great value for senior executives. Even if the executive does not take your inbound cold call, they will not throw out the book you sent them. Executives value business books, so turn these books into your business card to warm up your cold calls.

Postcard Method

Fortune 1000 Companies. It may be hard to believe, but postcards work well with management. They are quick to read, repetitive, inexpensive, and visible without having to open an envelope. Postcards should be larger in size (approximately 6 x 8 inches).

The front of the postcard should display your primary message. In order for your message to be read, it needs to be direct and straightforward, using as few words as possible. It needs to scream your sales value proposition at the senior executive.

On the back of the postcard, list the basic benefits of your sales value proposition and your telephone number. That's it. Send it every month. It will get noticed and will generate interest (maybe even a phone call) and provide a smoother introduction when you cold call.

Small Businesses. Post cards work for small businesses, too. Small business owners are more likely to read their own mail, which means your postcard will reach the president or owner.

How White Papers Can Be Used As Marketing and Sales Tools

Business-to-business (B2B) white papers are successful tools for marketing to management, when done correctly. They respond to the basic need of executives to read and understand value in a format they use themselves. White papers allow you to succinctly address management's objections in a non-vendor presentation method that will help move the sales cycle forward.

A good B2B white paper is likely to be passed on from one executive to another. When done incorrectly, a B2B white paper becomes more filler for the file that is emptied daily.

White papers are a waste of time if they discuss general benefits, features, or functions of the product or service but do not address the very reason(s) why management should buy. Additionally, white papers are a waste of time if they are too long.

How do you develop a B2B white paper that is interesting to management and helps you close more sales?

Develop white papers based on sales objections that senior executives give you on why they will not buy your product or service.

Sales Objection White Paper Guidelines

1. Collect and document the top twenty sales objections you hear from management prospects.

2. List the top five executive titles and categorize the sales objections by the business titles (e.g., VPs' sales objections, CFOs' sales objections).

3. Keep all white papers to a maximum of three pages.

4. Use the sales objection given to you by management in the title of the white paper.

5. Include the title of the executive who gave you the sales objection into the name of the white paper.

6. Insert the vertical industry that gave you this sales objection into the title of the white paper.

7. Use words from your senior executive dictionary in the white paper to communicate you are a peer.

8. Keep complex features and program descriptions to a minimum. Technical discourse scares most management. This white paper is NOT a technical paper.

9. Use a third-party research quote, graph, or business statistic in your white paper. It cannot come from you. It should be an industry-recognized authority that will make your white paper appear more independent in thought.

10. Discuss how the use of your product or service increases income, decreases expenses (directly or indirectly), or manages risks. Do not make direct references to your product or service, just indirect observations.

11. Develop both printed and electronic PDF copies of each white paper so you can hand it out and e-mail it to prospects.

12. Create content based on how to increase income, decrease expenses, or manage risks through the use of your product or service. Management buys products and services for these three reasons, so your white paper must focus on these needs.

Sales Objection White Paper Example 1

Business Vertical: Manufacturing Industry

Item Sold: Product—Capital Equipment

Buyer Title: Vice President of Plant Operations

Sales Objection: Can't afford it

White Paper Name: How Manufacturing Plant Operation Vice Presidents Can Reduce Business Costs By Outsourcing Capital Equipment Purchases!

Sales Objection White Paper Example 2

Business Vertical: Hospitality Industry

Item Sold: Product—Software

Buyer Title: Chief Financial Officer

Sales Objection: Already has software

White Paper Title: How Restaurant CFOs Can Increase Revenue Per Customer By Using The Right Suggestive Selling Software Application!

Sales Objection White Paper Example 3

Business Vertical: Healthcare Industry

Item Sold: Professional Services

Buyer Title: General Manager

Sales Objection: Not needed

White Paper Title: How Healthcare General Managers Can Reduce Daily Operating Costs By Using Third-Party Billing Services!

Why does this model work?

Most marketing material and brochures focus on the vendor's needs instead of the buyer's needs. This sales objection white paper approach is centralized on managing sales cycle objections using parallel imaging techniques.

A senior executive's attention is drawn to an article by its title. When a senior executive recognizes his position and industry in the title of the white paper, it is like a magnet that forces him to read it.

This marketing technique is even more effective when a manager reads the standard sales objections she gives to salespeople about why she has not bought their product or service.

This model of marketing is an effective technique for selling to management. Develop white papers for every sales objection you receive and for every executive you meet and you will sell more.

This works primarily because you are not acting like a vendor by sending management corporate brochures. Instead, you are sending specific titled information that responds to the sales objections they give salespeople. By inserting their title and the business vertical inside the title of the white paper, it psychologically encourages them to read the article.

How to Use Executive Seminars to Generate Prospects

Most product or service seminars are a waste of time. They attract supervisors who are professional lookers, attend in order to appear busy to their bosses, or want the free food some seminars and workshops offer.

To effectively develop a peer-to-peer networking environment for management, you must bypass the traditional *dog and pony show* where you display your offerings. Instead, focus on using the workshop as a way to educate targeted executives with information needed to help them increase their business success while simultaneously allowing salespeople to meet and greet their prospects in a non-vendor setting.

Executive seminars work well with senior executives of large international firms and presidents of small businesses. Executive seminars are an effective way to generate qualified leads for salespeople trying to sell to management.

Unfortunately, companies normally delegate executive seminars to their marketing departments, which develop a single theme and reproduce it on a regional basis to help the sales force. The problem with this approach is that it does not build rapport and client interaction for the sales team. It's a shotgun approach that generates some leads, but keeps moving as a traveling road show. It's easy for the marketing department to deploy, but reduces the seminar's overall effectiveness.

The most valuable lead-generating approach is to package your seminars and workshops in a **series of six sessions** in a particular geographic region, once a month for six consecutive months. By focusing a series of events within a specific geography (instead of traveling from city to city) you gain a recurring networking opportunity for salespeople. The key to marketing your seminars successfully is that these workshops or seminars *cannot* display, discuss, or present your product or service.

Vendors have product or service seminars. Peers have educational seminars focused on helping management see you as a pain management strategist.

The seminars should be by invitation only and the subject matter needs to be relevant to senior executives. By having a series of seminars, you invite the opportunity to continually bring back the same executives, as well as their peers, and establish you and your firm as a source of knowledge. And by making it an invitation only event, you will exclude unwanted competitors from attending and trolling for prospects.

Also, by packaging the seminars as a series for management executives, it allows you to sell sponsorships to non-competitive partners to help support your marketing expenses.

Theme. The uniqueness about executive seminars is the subliminal sell. Your seminar themes should be based on important issues facing your targeted prospects in their daily business cycle and should be related to how your sales value proposition can fix their pain.

Senior executives will attend if they feel your seminar has value. Name the seminar using the targeted prospect inside the title of the seminar (just like the white paper approach).

For example:

▶ Why CFOs Need to Manage Manufacturing
Production Costs at the Subcomponent Level

▶ How Vice Presidents of Marketing Can Increase
Customer Traffic to Their Web Site

▶ Five Ways Distribution CEOs Can Increase
Profits Immediately

Speakers. Never have your firm's management team participate as speakers. Your marketing department will push to have your team represented, since they are paying for the events, but this is a mistake. It is just ego reinforcement for your management team. Your firm is only to act as the event's *host*. You should schedule executives who are from non-competing companies to be your speakers. Your workshop will become a true educational seminar and roundtable discussion. Since it is your seminar, always have the speakers submit their presentations ahead of time to make sure they are succinct and to the point. Allow the speakers to market your program to their own databases, but again, only to senior executives. Try to coordinate your marketing with the speakers' marketing departments. Make sure that the speakers are talking generically at the seminar and *not* directly selling. **The way to get senior executives to attend your seminar is to have senior executives speak.**

Sponsors. The nice thing about having a series of executive seminars in the same city is that you can have other firms sponsor the costs. The way to do this is to sell executive sponsorships. The sponsoring company will get the attendee list after the presentation and have their name on the advertising, mailing, and signage. It is similar to a golf sponsorship. They get to meet and mingle under the entertainment tent for the price of an ad. Sponsors will usually volunteer to speak, so make sure they are the right fit. If you sell sponsorships, you can sell them individually for each seminar or as a package for the complete series.

Marketing. Prior to locking in the dates of your seminar series, confirm with the local chamber of commerce and print media that there are no competing events, including sports and civic functions, already scheduled.

You should shoot for a 1-5% attendance based on your mailing list. If you have a compelling reason for people to attend the seminars, like industry managers discussing current issues and concerns, they will come.

Having held multiple executive seminars and managed marketing departments responsible for their implementation, I have come to the conclusion that the best method to generate attendance is the following, in *descending* order:

1. Personalized mailed invitations (like a wedding invitation)

2. Opt-in e-mail

3. Speakers' prospect mailing lists

4. Press releases

5. Print advertising

Your seminar series should be marketed at least **two months prior** to the first actual seminar date. All invitations need to request an RSVP. All RSVPs should be confirmed with a follow-up letter, seminar itinerary, and speakers' bios. One week before the seminar date, reconfirm all RSVPs with another letter (or by e-mail).

Scheduling. I have found that Tuesdays and Wednesdays are the best for executive seminars. There is a big debate on what time your seminar should be held. Some say breakfast meetings, other say during the day, and yet others say early evening.

The most successful executive seminars I have held were from 6:00 p.m. to 8:00 p.m. and served finger food.

Below is the agenda that I have successfully used:

6:00 p.m. - 6:30 p.m.   Social time/food served

6:30 p.m.   I ring a bell to indicate the seminar is about to start

6:30 p.m. - 6:45 p.m.   Host makes welcoming comments and introduces speakers

6:45 p.m. - 8:00 p.m.   Speaker roundtable discussions/audience questioning

Pulling it all together. Below is the format that has helped me execute my management seminars smoothly:

1.   Have your support staff seated at a table at the entrance of the seminar location to sign-in invited guests and to hand out preprinted badges. Business cards are also collected in a fish bowl.

2.   Always have a handout describing the hosting company, the sponsors, the speakers' backgrounds, and the panel discussion format.

3.   Have a table at the entrance (near the food) to display your sponsors' (and your) marketing materials.

4.   When the seminar starts, the host stands at a podium on stage or in front of the audience.

5.   The host will introduce himself, the sponsors, the host company, their sales value proposition, and the panel speakers.

6.   The host will ask questions to the panel and the panel responds.

7.   An overhead slide show is used only for panel introductions and brief subject matter review only. (Slide show presentations with a panel talking freely can be distracting to the audience.)

8.   During the introductions, remind the audience of the next scheduled seminar date and the subject matter to be discussed.

9.   The panel is seated at a long table on stage with bottled water or glasses of water.

10.   Never schedule more than three speakers for the panel.

11.   Ask the panel to submit questions ahead of time to the host that are relevant to the seminar subject matter.

12.   Resubmit all potential questions for the panel to alert them to questions that may be asked.

13. Place two standing microphones in the audience to allow for audience participation and questioning.

14. At the end of the discussion, thank everyone for coming and remind them of the next seminar date.

15. If a supervisor requests to come to your seminar, tell them it is for management only and please have their manager send you an e-mail appointing them as their corporate replacement.

Networking. When using this marketing method, your networking opportunities are at their highest level during the social time before the workshop starts. This is when your sales team should be meeting and greeting management on a one-to-one basis. The goal here is to interact as a peer-to-peer, not overwhelm with a sales attack.

By having a series of monthly events, you allow your sales team to begin building initial introductions into networked qualified management prospects.

> ## Case Study—Generating Leads: Executive Seminar
>
> Several years ago, I was working with a small startup consulting company that wanted to meet and sell management of Fortune 1000 clients. We held a series of monthly executive seminars in one city by invitation only. Using the networking format described, we were able to sell executive marketing sponsorships for $200,000—more than enough to pay for the marketing.
>
> During the social time, the executive sponsor had its business development staff out in full force, shaking hands and making introductions to all of the management attendees.
>
> The consulting company averaged 140 people per seminar with more than 90% being a senior executive. Since this was a startup company, it launched their name, their brand, and their revenue stream while someone else paid for the marketing.
>
> For small business sales, this is a great way for you to dominate a regional territory. By partnering with other small business suppliers and service providers like accountants, lawyers, and consultants, you can easily cover the cost of your seminars and marketing while developing new customers and prospects for all.

What Is Engagement Marketing™ and How Does It Shorten Your Sales Cycle?

Selling to management is a sport. It requires you to train and constantly prepare for your time on the field. However, before you can play, you have to be invited to the game.

One of the key ways to successfully sell to executives is to have your firm's name in front of the decision makers on a regular basis until they are ready to buy. Value Forward Selling uses an automated touch program that sends marketing messages to your target market on a regular basis.

We call this *Engagement Marketing*™ and use it ourselves to create a continuous inbound flood of qualified management leads. Engagement Marketing works because buying cycles and sales cycles are always different. If you carry a sales quota, this can be a problem. To shorten your sales cycle, you must constantly engage management prospects with reasons why they need your product or service and how its usage will help them in their daily jobs. If you were to send them traditional marketing material, they would just ignore it.

The goal of Engagement Marketing is to position your firm as an industry knowledge center so prospects see your products and services as tools to help them fix their business pains. Figure 2 helps to visualize how Engagement Marketing can shorten your sales cycle.

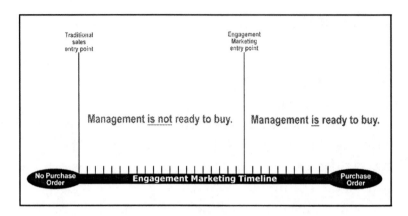

Figure 2.   ***Engagement Marketing™ Timeline.*** This timeline shows two entry points—the traditional sales entry point and the Engagement Marketing™ entry point. The traditional sales cycle starts at the beginning of the timeline where the salesperson must go through the entire sales cycle. The entry point of Engagement Marketing™ starts halfway through the traditional sales cycle, at the point where the prospect has already decided to buy and is qualified before contacting you.

When using Engagement Marketing™, management prospects who are in the non-buying zone are coddled with business content that moves them forward to the buying zone based on their increased education of how your product or service can help them increase revenue, decrease expenses, or manage risks. This is accomplished by delivering valuable content through various mediums that are non-traditional marketing channels. **That's right, non-traditional marketing channels.**

The moment management prospects think you are selling to them, you lose credibility and eliminate your ability to educate why they should buy from you. Engagement Marketing™ is based on communicating business content and value on a regular basis that is focused on your prospect's needs. It will stimulate the prospect to shorten their buying cycle based on a better understanding of how your product or service helps them.

This process positions you and your firm as pain management specialists and you become seen as a business peer rather than a vendor trying to force-feed a purchaser. Once prospects see you as a knowledge center, they forget you are a vendor and seek out your help.

So, how does Engagement Marketing™ work?

By developing and delivering strong business content on how your targeted prospects can become more successful in their jobs, you subtly nudge their thought process to become more educated buyers—and educated buyers buy more quickly.

This information is delivered in the form of teleseminars, eNewsletters, webinars, public workshops and specific targeted white papers. They are deployed on a monthly basis allowing you to move non-buying management prospects closer to the buying cycle by feeding them a continuous source of business value. It is a tool to prod prospects to make faster purchases.

Once a month, you need to touch the prospect. Prospects generally have their own buy cycle, which, in most cases, does not parallel your sales cycle. So, by keeping your firm's name in front of them on a consistent basis, you have a better chance of having them contact you when they are ready to buy because your firm is on the top of their mind.

This is a passive lead-generation process. Set it up with your marketing department, an outside firm, or do it yourself and then wait for the leads to pour in.

How to Use Channel Partners and Networking to Build Your Pipeline

No product or service sales training program can be effective unless the discussion involves the subject of business networking. As mentioned earlier, by networking with management (and people who interact with management), your ability to penetrate large and small accounts will be greatly enhanced. Simultaneously, knowing the executive through local association meetings enables you to eliminate competition quickly. Clients (particularly those involved in the largest company purchases of $2,000,000 and above) still want to *respect* their sales rep.

One of the quickest ways to increase the amount of leads you generate is through your current strategic partners. This works with both small businesses and Fortune 1000 companies.

Fortune 1000 Companies. Partnering with the individual channel reps of your company's current strategic partners (in your local territory) takes time, an expense account, and mutual lead sharing. It is important to spend time with local partner reps. Most channel partner managers have multiple relationships in a specific region, so they have many options to choose from when offering leads. The more they get to know you, the more apt they are to share leads.

Other areas of networking include:

- Chamber of commerce business meetings

- Local business meetings

- Local "meet and greet" meetings sponsored by business publications

Small Businesses. If you currently sell to small businesses consisting of more than ten employees, you have a great opportunity for a tremendous amount of leads through local partnerships. These partnerships will not happen unless you get out and introduce yourself. When appropriate, offer a 10% finders' fee

(based on collection) to anyone who introduces you to
a prospect that generates revenue.

Imagine how many small business leads you might
have if you partnered with even two from each of the
following categories:

- Accountants

- Lawyers

- Business insurance agents

- Chamber of commerce members

- Local lead clubs

- Local toastmaster clubs

- Local computer hardware companies

- Local software companies

- Business consultants

- Local college professors (especially community
  colleges)

- Commercial real estate agents

- Local church groups

- Local advertising firms

- Local printers

These groups are involved in the community on a daily basis. They know whose business is growing, whose business is adding staff, and what each president or key contact's name is. If you partner with just two contacts in each of these categories, you will have more leads than you can handle. Meet with them personally, explain what your firm does, show examples of your work if appropriate, and then put them on your mailing list. Buy them lunch and spread the word.

How to Use the Touch Management Program to Communicate With Your Prospects

This part of marketing occurs after you have completed your first meeting (discussed in Chapter 6) and scheduled additional meetings with the senior executive. If you've made it this far with the senior executive, you need to keep them near and dear to you as the principal decision maker in your sales process *and* an excellent business coach. Use ongoing communication to *your* advantage to *take* advantage during the prospect's buying cycle.

Under the **Touch Management Program**, you contact every person you meet during the sales cycle program **once a week**. To accomplish this, I recommend you have your marketing team develop a series of customer contact devices that can be sent to each contact you are currently negotiating with. The Touch Management Program differs from other periodic marketing efforts in that it is designed specifically to be delivered **DURING THE SALES CYCLE** on a weekly basis to existing prospects (e.g., a press release, a pre-developed sales letter, or a business case study).

The goal is to touch every person within that prospect company every week with your name and your firm's name, along with your marketing message throughout the sales cycle.

This is a light Touch Management Program in that you are not personally calling every day to present; rather your marketing team presents for you. This program does not absolve you of the responsibility to follow up in person each week, but it helps you bridge the time between personal meetings by connecting you to the prospect consistently during the sales cycle timeline.

When using the Touch Management Program between the first and second meetings, if you are sending letters to managers you were directed to work with by your management contact, always send a copy to the senior executive, and indicate as such on any correspondence to keep her informed about your ongoing communication with her company. Copying the senior executive will help you keep the dialogue open and direct between you and the executive.

Noting the proliferation of rapid communication technologies, including cell phones, e-mail, and pagers, it's surprising to see how many basic sales skills are still missing from professional salespeople. Use the Touch Management Program to build your sales skills and communicate regularly with the executive.

Review and Exercises

1. Make a list of ten senior executives that you would like to meet. Visit your local bookstore or favorite online bookstore and select a newly released business book that would be appropriate for the prospects you want to reach. Make sure you take time to read the book, scan it thoroughly, or read extensive reviews of the book to avoid sending something that might offend the prospect. Draft an inscription so you have an opportunity to read it over several times before you write it inside the book. Send the book out to your ten prospects and make a note in your calendar to cold call them in seven days.

2. Develop at least four white papers using the following guidelines:

    a. Write down at least eight sales objections you hear from prospects.

    b. List the top five executive titles and categorize the sales objections by the business titles.

    c. Develop the title of the white paper using the title of the manager who gives you

the sales objection, the industry vertical,
and the item you are trying to sell.

d. Use third-party research for quotes,
graphs, or statistics.

e. When drafting your white paper, discuss
how your product or service increases
revenue, decreases expenses, or manages
risks without being too obvious.

f. Keep your white paper to a maximum of
three pages.

g. Use words from your senior executive
dictionary.

h. Develop both printed and electronic
PDF copies of your white paper.

3. Attend several networking events in your area.
After each meeting, keep a spiral notebook
handy to jot down notes of people you met,
information you received about industry events,
corporate changes, and any tips that might help
you develop your pipeline, craft an alternate
sales value proposition, or write a white paper.
If you listen closely, you should be able to pick
up on information relevant to your marketing
needs, visual value development, and sales
opportunities.

4. If you have a marketing department, have them design a postcard targeting a specific sales objection. You will want to provide a draft of the body and possibly the tag line for your marketing department to use and/or revise. If you are developing the postcard yourself, ask your peers to review the postcard for their immediate reaction. In your postcard, make sure you put a "call to action" step (i.e., download your white paper for free). Send the postcard to your prospect list. You may want to take this a step further and develop a series of postcards on one or more sales objections and mail them on an evenly spaced timeline (i.e., every two weeks).

Chapter 4
Generating Leads: Marketing to Management

Chapter 5

Generating Leads: Cold Calling Management

After reading this chapter, you will know:

- The goal of cold calling

- How to develop your telemarketing script

- How to handle cold calling sales objections

- How to manage gatekeepers

Cold calling separates a professional salesperson making $500,000 a year from everyone else. If you cannot or will not cold call, you will not make large sums of money. *Hunters always cold call.*

Cold calling is the fastest way to increase your sales pipeline, your company's revenue, and your personal income. It is the difference between making a meeting with a CFO of a Fortune 500 company and selling to supervisors. If you were to analyze the top income sales positions in the U.S. (stockbrokers, commercial insurance salespeople, merger and acquisitions salespeople) you would find that they all cold call. **People who cold call are always better**

salespeople. Why? Because when salespeople cold call, they set up more meetings, which provides them more opportunities to practice their sales presentation and, ultimately, close more deals.

If you are one of those account managers who waits for the marketing department to send you leads, it is unlikely you will ever be the top salesperson in your company.

Let's be honest—you hate cold calling. It is labor intensive, it wears you down, and if you use the wrong techniques, it does not work.

So, you'd rather have the marketing department give you sales leads. But in our practice with sales teams, most marketing departments never generate enough qualified management leads.

Why aren't salespeople more successful at cold calling?

We know senior executives have telephones on their desks. Therefore, if they are not taking your phone call, then you are probably not communicating the right message.

Most cold calling techniques scare away prospects and gatekeepers because salespeople say the wrong words, flagging the receiver with vendor words and showing no business respect for the prospects they are phoning.

▶ Executives buy houses.

▶ Executives buy stocks and bonds.

▶ Executives buy insurance.

Senior executives are accustomed to inbound salespeople pitching their products and services. This continuous volume of inbound cold calls has created an instantaneous barrier by all management to any salesperson who sounds like a vendor. So, when salespeople use the same cold calling process over and over, they fail.

Selling to management requires you to show respect. Sounding like an insurance agent or stockbroker pitching today's hot deal is not going to get you a positive response.

The following are four reasons why cold calling is still the best way to consistently generate qualified management leads:

1. Cold calling allows you to shorten your sales cycle by casting a big net into the marketplace and leapfrogging into your competition's sales cycle as it happens. No matter how long your sales cycle is, when you cold call management,

you find concurrent sales cycles which are already underway by your competition that you can jump into. For example, if your average sales cycle is four months and you cold called into a competitor's sales cycle that had been underway for two months, you just reduced your sales cycle by two months.

2. When done correctly, cold calling is a scalable, replicable sales process that can be expanded to all salespeople. It allows sales teams to penetrate markets globally.

3. Cold calling directly to management by the salespeople without using a third-party intermediary (like an inside sales team or an outsourced telemarketing firm) immediately connects the calling salesperson with the targeted prospect and allows for instant peer-to-peer communication. Cold calling directly is a non-buffered communication method.

4. Cold calling increases the sales skills of salespeople by helping them practice their communication, objection, and value positioning with the most important person they can reach—the executive buyer.

The Goal of Cold Calling

Cold calling has only one goal—setting up a new meeting with the qualified buyer. It is not designed for you to gab away at how great your product or service is or to close prospects on the phone.

Your first cold call should last *no longer than 7 or 8 minutes*. If it goes longer, you are selling and you lose.

Our cold calling techniques are designed to entice the prospect to meet with you at a later date or schedule a specific conference call to discuss your products or services.

I know you will be tempted to hang on the phone with the senior executive once you get through the first time, but he is not ready to listen (even if he says he is) and you just end up burning your opportunity.

When you cold call and get through to a senior executive, it is a combination of what you say, luck, and timing. It's important that they are ready to listen, with no distractions, when you are ready to talk.

Don't jump sales steps by delivering a soliloquy on how great your service or product is. Instead, focus on the goal of the cold call, which is setting up a twenty-minute meeting to chat.

Remember, selling management is a step-by-step process of premeditated steps.

How to Develop Your Telemarketing Script

The best way to make telemarketing work is seeing the results of your efforts. This means scheduling meetings with qualified decisions makers; e.g., meeting with a VP in a Fortune 1000 company to discuss buying your new product, or talking with a CEO of a small bike manufacturing company to discuss a strategy and branding concept for her resellers.

Before you can write your telemarketing script, you need to develop your sales value proposition. As explained in Chapter 2, make sure your sales value proposition answers or responds to your target prospect's problems or pain. Selling products or services successfully to management means you must become a doctor. You need to find the business pain and then fix it by closing the sale.

The following telemarketing script works only with management. Supervisors will not respond to this script because it does not appeal to their needs. This script works with management because it uses psychology and peer association, and accelerates their need to know what their competitors are doing.

9 Steps to Develop Your Management Telemarketing Script

Use these steps in sequence. <u>Do not jump steps</u> because it will not be as effective.

Step 1. **Provide a personal introduction:** *Hello, this is Paul DiModica.*

This shows that you are a professional. Always give your full name and ask for the executive <u>by his/her full name</u>. This shows respect. Only unprofessional salespeople ask for prospects by their first name when they have never spoken with them before.

Step 2. **Offer a professional courtesy:** *Thanks for taking my call.*

Again, it shows respect, like a peer.

Step 3. **Provide your sales value proposition:** *We are Milestone Management Specialists for the manufacturing industry.*

Use the methods previously discussed to help prospects *visualize* how you can fix their business pain.

Step 4. **Position that you are at the right title level and have the right to speak with them as a**

peer. Insert their title into your pitch: *We work only with CFOs of manufacturing companies such as yourself.*

Psychologically, it communicates you are equal and shows respect. It also creates a need of the prospect to know who else you have talked with.

Step 5. **Describe the pain your sales value proposition fixes:** *Through our programs and services, we help CFOs of manufacturing companies reduce operating production expenses and deliver production runs on time and on budget.*

Once you have developed your SVP, you must develop a two-line sentence that describes how your product or service increases income, decreases expenses, or manages risks. Then insert it here in Step 5.

Step 6. **Name drop references and equal prospect titles:** *We work with other CFOs of manufacturing companies like Company X, Company Y, and Company Z.*

In this step, you entice the prospect by providing other companies who have made a business decision to work with your firm and

again carefully communicate that you are a
peer and only work with titles like his/hers.

Step 7. **Optional: Identify your company's name:** *I
am calling from the ABC firm.*

NOTE: You'll notice that during the beginning
of these cold calling steps, I did not say my
company name. **Company names get in the
way of selling to a new (and sometimes
existing) management prospect.** Why?
Because they paint *visual brochures* that often
confuse prospects of your value. Hold back
before you reveal your company name and
you will be more successful. Value first—
company name second.

You may be concerned about not giving your
company name out immediately (especially if
you work in a big Fortune 1000 company), but
by now, you have thrown out enough value
that hopefully the prospect will not make a
judgment based on your company's name.
(This is Value Forward Marketing™.) If you
want to say your company name, now is the
time.

Step 8. **Ask for a small amount of time:** *Can we meet for twenty minutes to chat, to see if our programs and services are a good fit for your firm?*

If you are succinct in your sales approach, you can qualify any prospect in less than twenty minutes. Twenty minutes is a reasonable amount of time to ask any executive to share. Asking for one hour is excessive when they don't know you. Twenty minutes is respectful.

Step 9. **Confirm that you value their time:** *I will not waste your time.*

Management prospects think you are going to waste their time, no matter what you tell them. Because of this fear, you need to proactively communicate that you understand this concern and are here to respect their time.

Each one of these steps is important. They communicate who you are, what makes you and your firm different, why you are calling, and show you respect the executive's time. Use this format and you will be able to meet the decision maker.

Fortune 1000 Companies. If you are selling to management at Fortune 1000 companies, some telemarketing methods ask you to probe the contact on the first phone call to determine the business opportunity.

Let's be honest. You are not going to cold call the senior vice president of operations of the nation's largest supermarket chain and begin the call by probing about his business needs and what his current business issues are. He doesn't know you. **He is not going to start telling you about his business pains.** Why? Because you have not yet earned the right.

This is a disrespectful way to talk to management that comes from old sales training methods taught by people who never sold to management. The truth is, when selling products or services to management of a Fortune 1000 company or a small business, you need to do some research before you try to sell to them. You should understand their business pain before you call.

If you are a sales manager in a growth directed company, focus on having your salespeople call directors and above. Remember, no matter how big the company is, managers and supervisors almost never have the authority to sign off on business proposals. Even if they tell you it is their decision, ultimately they will have to ask their boss. Another interesting observation in management sales is that **supervisors never send you up to their boss; they only push you down to their subordinates.**

When was the last time a manager of purchasing or operations said to you, *Paul, this is amazing! I'm going to introduce you to my boss, the VP.*

It doesn't happen often.

Either they bring your opportunity directly to their boss and try to make themselves look good, or they send you to George, the assistant supervisor, a management level lower. Either way, you lose. The supervisor is not as good a salesperson as you are, and will likely communicate your message in the wrong way to the VP. Worse, you are stuck with George who cannot make any decisions.

Always sell up—the higher, the better. If you have crafted your sales value proposition correctly, you should be able to call a senior executive and get her attention. Having a CFO send you down to the vice president of operations is a whole lot better than talking to George, the assistant supervisor.

Case Study—Generating Leads: Selling Up The Org Chart (Fortune 1000 Product Sale)

Some time ago, I taught an experienced director of business development how to cold call the CEO of a Fortune 1000 company. After we developed a personalized sales value proposition script, he called the CEO's administrator and left a message with her.

The CEO's secretary called back and said the CEO was interested and wanted the salesperson to call the senior VP of marketing. The account manager called the senior VP of marketing and told him that the CEO was interested and that he was instructed to call

---

him to set up a meeting to chat. Of course, the senior VP of marketing said yes.

If the salesperson had called lower in the organizational chart, he may never have gotten the chance to meet the senior VP of marketing.

A lead or a contact should not be considered a qualified prospect unless they have a title of a ***director or above***. If you follow this method, you will always sell more.

Go for the heavy hitters and you will become a heavy hitter.

Case Study—Generating Leads: Service Firm

A service company I consulted with had been cold calling the director of marketing of a local 25-person business without much success. I suggested they call the CEO with a special sales value proposition. They did and got a meeting.

Many times, in both large and small companies, lower-level managers who are motivated by politics often prevent you from getting to the decision maker.

Additionally, sometimes a sales value proposition is intellectually over the heads of lower-level employees. Senior executives of any size firm generally have broader knowledge about their business and operational needs than department supervisors.

Stop wasting your time with low-level manager titles. **Sell up, never down.**

Cold Calling FAQs

Q: **When is the best time to cold call?**

A: All day.

ભ   ભ   ભ

Q: **When will you have the best opportunity to speak with senior executives?**

A: Before 8:00 a.m. and after 5:30 p.m. because the senior executive's assistant is usually not in the office at this time and the boss usually picks up his or her own phone. Saturdays also work well. Also, calling at 10 minutes before the hour will work well for reaching executives because they are often getting ready for the next meeting.

ભ   ભ   ભ

The smart way to cold call on the phone is by purchasing a targeted database of your prospects from a list company and loading it into a contact manager like *Act!, Gold Mine, SalesForce.com* or *SalesLogix.*

Then make *at least thirty phone calls each day* three times a week prospecting for new business. The best way to cold call is to schedule calling time in your appointment book—like any meeting.

You might be wondering how you are going to make *thirty* phone calls a day. Trust me, you will not reach thirty people each day. Eighty percent of the time you will speak with gatekeepers (their assistants) or get their voice-mail. The other 20 percent of the time, you will be touching prospects, and with prospecting comes increased revenue and increased commissions. (Remember, only call directors or above.)

CB   CB   CB

Q: **How many companies should you call?**

A: Based on your market, you should load between 300 and 500 companies into your database. By calling thirty companies a day three days a week, you will end up contacting many of your database prospects once a month.

CB   CB   CB

Cold calling's immediate effects:

1. Increases the size of your sales pipeline.

2. Increases your communication sales skills by repeatedly practicing your verbal techniques over and over.

3. Enables you to shorten your sales cycle by falling into and interrupting competitors' sales cycles.

4. Enables you to increase the number of meetings you get with prospects.

5. Enables you to negotiate better with clients because now you have multiple deals closing at the same time.

Keep in mind, most of your competitors do not like to cold call.

Here is an interesting side effect of cold calling: If there are five salespeople in your company, and each person calls 300 companies a month, that's *1,500 companies* hearing your name and getting your marketing message every month.

That's called advertising and branding!

Another benefit of cold calling is that you get better at selling. The more you talk to clients, the more confidence you'll have and the better your closing ratio will be.

By implementing a cold calling program, your sales will go up.

How to Handle Cold Calling Sales Objections

Telemarketing Dos and Don'ts

1. When telemarketing to senior executives, **never sell your product or service over the phone on the first call**. Your primary goal is to **sell a twenty-minute meeting**. Management teams do not buy immediately. Instead, they buy **pain relievers** to help them get through the day. This meeting can be in person or another conference call at a later date. Never explain what you do in detail on the first call. Your entire communication time on the phone with the executive should **be five minutes, no longer than eight,** including the time for them to schedule a meeting at a later date.

2. If the executive starts asking you detailed questions about your service or product, push back and say, *There's far more detail than I can give you in five minutes on the phone. Let's set up a meeting (or a telephone conference call) so I can explain in person. I will not waste your time.*

3. Be confident. Don't be apprehensive. Executives are very busy. They will speak to you if you are confident and can help them be more successful in their jobs.

4. When writing a product or service telemarketing script, always include the line: *We specialize in [INSERT YOUR SALES VALUE PROPOSITION] and are working with [INSERT THE TITLE OF THE PERSON YOU ARE SPEAKING TO]*. The reason for this is that it validates to the gatekeepers and executives they are the proper title and management level you should be speaking to and you are a peer (e.g., *We work with CFOs, We work with VPs of Ops, We work with presidents of small companies*, etc.).

   Add value to your client. You are there to help them become more successful. You are not calling to chat about sports, the weather, or the economy. You are calling them to fix their business pain. This pain could be a lack of revenue, poor inventory turns on their sales, an expensive HR software system, out-of-control construction costs, or a boss who is angry with them because competitors are taking away market share.

5. One of the biggest mistakes most salespeople make is they do not plan their actions. Don't say to yourself, *Well, I guess I'll call Paul today because I haven't spoken with him in three weeks.* Instead, plot why you are calling Paul and what your goal is when you talk to him. **Always have a goal.** Be premeditated in your selling process.

6. When leaving a message on the voice-mail of a senior executive, use the same script, but do not leave your firm's name. Many times company names get in the way of selling and it will scare qualified prospects. If your company is well-known, then the prospect is likely to make a judgment and not call you back based on your brand's visual brochure. Or, if your company's name tells the prospect what product or service you sell, again they will ignore your voice-mail (e.g., XYS Wholesale Company, IT Project Work, XYZ Corporate Consulting, etc.).

Try to have the prospect call you back on your direct line or extension and state your telephone number twice in the message. If they reach your voice-mail upon returning your call, make sure your recording identifies your name, but not your firm's name. The reason you do not leave your firm's name is that you prevent the prospect from developing a preconceived opinion based on your firm's name. The end result is that you will be trading phone calls and maintaining their intrigue of the pain management stated in your SVP. Management prospects will call you back if your sales value proposition helps them fix their business pain. Intrigue them with your sales value proposition.

For example, if a tree falls on my company's office and you called me and said, *my firm specializes in tree removal,* I would return your call from voice-mail, because you are prepared to help me fix the business pain. If prospects are not returning your voice-mail calls, then your message is not intriguing enough about the pain you fix. Review your SVP. Don't confuse them with your company brand.

Fortune 1000 Companies. Depending on how your sales territory is set up (national, vertical, or local), you may be calling to set up your first meeting as a conference call or an on-site meeting to discuss your sales value proposition.

1. Cold call the senior executive (CEO, CFO, CIO, etc.).

2. Talk with him/her for eight minutes or less to develop interest or direction.

3. Set up a twenty-minute meeting, either on-site or via phone conference.

4. Meet for twenty minutes to validate they are qualified. Mine for opportunities. Before you leave, schedule another meeting.

5. At the end of the twenty-minute meeting, set up a new meeting for one hour to focus on opportunities/proposals (an executive briefing).

6. Request to present to as many decision influencers as possible.

Case Study—Generating Leads: Fortune 1000 Telemarketing Script

I worked with a company that sold Balanced Scorecard software and consulting services. The Balanced Scorecard is a Fortune 1000 strategy and measurement process used by senior executive teams. The software company was having a hard time reaching senior executives because the CIOs didn't understand it and the CFOs kept pushing the salespeople back to the CIOs because they were selling software.

Below is the telemarketing script we used:

Good day, my name is Paul DiModica. Thank you for taking my call. We are specialists in the CFO Balanced Scorecard (or CIO Scorecard) and I am calling you to see if we can chat about potentially using a scorecarding methodology in your firm to increase corporate profitability. Companies like Company X use our services. I am calling from the XYZ firm.

Immediately, this company's ability to get past the gatekeepers and reach the CFO increased dramatically.

Once, when I was testing the script, I had an executive secretary say, *Well I don't think he is the right person since this is software.* I responded, *Yes, he is the right person. He is the CFO, correct?* When she responded yes, I then said, *Well, this is the CFO Scorecard and we only work with CFOs.* She immediately transferred me to her boss. Don't let gatekeepers intimidate you. You are only doing your job.

Ask for a twenty-minute meeting. This way, the executive will feel he/she is in control when you meet (or chat again). Remember, it is important to be confident, but subservient, to the executive's ego so you can get the meeting. Arrogance never works with executives.

Always say you want to *chat.* It is a passive request to meet and it will lower the protective walls that automatically rise when they speak with salespeople.

Make sure your talking points and objection responses are handy when you start to call. Always be prepared. *Never shoot from the hip.*

Small Businesses. When cold calling small businesses with less than twenty employees, get in your car and drive around. Walk into their office and ask for the owner. Be friendly. If the secretary asks why you want to meet the owner, tell her you were in the area and wanted to introduce yourself to him or her for five minutes. If the secretary does not get the president or call that person on the phone to see if they are available, ask if you could set up a twenty-minute meeting at a later date.

If the owner is not available and the secretary will not schedule a meeting with the owner for the future, leave some information and call back later.

If the owner comes out, just say you were in the area and ask if they have five minutes to chat. After five minutes, set up a meeting, thank them, and be on your way.

Accepting that no one likes to cold call means it must be hard to do. Riding a bike was hard to do in the beginning as well. After you practice and get the hang of it (and the success of it), you will see value and will use cold calling as part of your selling arsenal.

My recommendation to anyone selling products or services to the small business market is that you should focus on firms with ten or more employees. The smaller the company, the more sales maintenance you will have.

1. Cold call the president.

2. Talk with him or her for eight minutes or less to develop interest for a meeting.

3. Focus on how you will increase revenue, decrease expenses, or manage risks.

4. Set up a twenty-minute meeting either on-site or via phone conference.

5. Meet for twenty minutes, validate why you should be there, and mine for opportunities. Before you finish, schedule another meeting.

6. Develop a proposal, deliver it in person, and close the deal.

Any deal under $30,000 should take no more than two on-site meetings to close.

> ## Case Study—Generating Leads: Telemarketing Script for Business Services
>
> Here is a script for a design service targeting small businesses:
>
> > *Hello my name is Paul DiModica. Thank you for taking my call. We are Business Development Specialists and we work with CEOs like yourself in the wholesale industry to help them develop and implement professional communication programs to increase revenue.*
> >
> > *I am calling from the ABC firm. Companies like Company X, Company Y, and Company Z currently use our services.*
> >
> > *I am calling to see if you and I can meet for twenty minutes to chat about our services and some of your firm's needs. I will not waste your time and I will discuss with you how we can increase your company's revenue.*

Caveat for Small Business Selling. What is your time worth? My experience and our clients' experiences selling products and services to small businesses is that you have to determine how small to go. I have found that small businesses with less than ten employees are usually higher maintenance. Typically the management team is primarily the owners, and the budgets are so tight they will extend your sales cycle as they try to wheel and deal with your proposal price. Since your time is valuable, you may want to determine a minimum price point, such as $3,000 or $5,000, as an entry point of what you sell. Of course, there are exceptions to everything and well-managed businesses with a professional management team or a small startup with three employees may still buy $200,000 of products or professional services from you. However, this is usually the exception instead of the rule when you get below the magic line of demarcation of ten employees.

How to Manage Gatekeepers

When trying to sell to senior executives of both small and large companies, you will invariably hit the company gatekeeper. In small companies, this may be the receptionist. In large firms, this is usually an executive assistant who is responsible for keeping people like you out. But you can, and will, get past most of them using the following methods.

Friend Method. When you call a large company, one method to get past the gatekeeper is to introduce yourself to them, and treat them as if they were the executive. Give them the courtesy of explaining what you do, what your sales value proposition is, and ask if they could assist you in setting up a twenty-minute phone conference with their boss.

I-am-a-Peer Method. If the gatekeeper will not help you and tries to pawn you off to some other executive, say politely, but confidently, *Our firm only works with [INSERT THE EXECUTIVE'S TITLE] and our customers include Company X, Company Y, and Company Z. I appreciate your direction but Mr./Ms. [INSERT THE EXECUTIVE'S NAME] is the right person I need to speak with.*

The Bribe Method. If multiple attempts to get through the gatekeeper have failed, send a book to the executive (and the gatekeeper) with an inscription inside such as, *Dear Mr. /Ms. X, I know you are very busy, but I thought you might enjoy this book. If you have a chance, let's chat.* I have successfully used this method many times with Fortune 1000 executives. After you send the book(s), call back and ask the assistant if their boss received it. Then ask again if she can help you set up a twenty-minute phone conference.

Only-A-Secretary Method. If the assistant asks you for details on what you do (so she can make a judgment call for her boss), speak firmly, lower your voice and say, *I apologize. I do not mean to be rude, but my company only works with [INSERT THEIR TITLE]. Do you personally make those kinds of decisions? If not, then I would like to speak with Mr./Ms. [INSERT THE EXECUTIVE'S NAME].*

Mini-Boss Method. When you encounter a gatekeeper who insists she knows what her boss wants, you have a secretary taking on the image of a boss. When you hear this objection, respond, *Ms. Secretary, I am surprised that your boss would not be interested. We work with other CFOs (CIOs, VPs, General Manager, etc.) at firms like Company X, Company Y and Company Z. Why is he not interested?*

Once they give you a reason (which they will make up) ask again for the twenty-minute meeting saying you will not waste their boss's time.

Pain-Reliever Method. When a secretary says, *Please send your information and Mr. X will follow up if he is interested;* respond, *Ms. Secretary, we specialize in [INSERT YOUR SALES VALUE PROPOSITION] and many of our relationships with [INSERT THE EXECUTIVE'S TITLE] are personalized based on their corporate needs. I would like to send you some general information and then call you back next Tuesday to see if this meets Mr. X's needs and warrants a twenty-minute conversation.*

Voice-Mail Method. If you consistently reach the executive's voice-mail, prepare a voice-mail script. A voice-mail telemarketing script based on your sales value proposition works great. I have had salespeople get over 40% returned calls from senior executives who were left a message. Why? Because they leave an intriguing value proposition on the voice-mail. The executive wants to know more and calls back.

03   03   03

Q: **How often should you call?**

A: That is a decision you will have to make based on your business opportunity costs. I have called a prospect ten times in one day (without leaving messages) to set up a meeting in order to close a deal, and once a week for forty-seven weeks to present a seven-figure opportunity. If you call multiple times in one week, **never** leave more than one voice-mail message. If you leave more than one message a week the client will think you are a pest. There have been multiple studies done showing that the average salesperson gets to the prospect usually between the fifth and seventh call. Be persistent. It may be your job, but don't be obnoxious.

Remember, if cold calling is not working for you, then maybe you are not communicating your value in your script. Senior executives have telephones on their desks and they do take calls. They are just not taking *your* calls. Review your sales value proposition to see if it stimulates an action step by the executive you are phoning.

⚃ ⚃ ⚃

Objection Management Equals Meetings

No matter how good your telemarketing script is, you will receive objections. In fact, you want the executive to ask questions because it shows you have their attention and they are listening.

The key to cold calling is to sell the first meeting, not the product or service. To do this, you need to walk a fine line of giving basic information and complete disclosure of why you are calling. Intrigue them with the concept that you are there to help relieve their problems or issues. Again, focus on the results your product or service delivers, not your product or service. Become a *consequence management specialist* helping senior executives fix business problems.

Because telemarketing objections lead to meetings, you need to create your script ahead of time. Below are several objections I have received along with the responses I developed for sales value propositions. These are objection scripts that have been successful.

Objection No. 1: *What do you mean, you are Milestone Management Specialists?*

Response: *What we do is help management teams review and plot strategic steps to implement their contractual milestones based on their business contracts and what I would like to do is meet with you for twenty minutes to chat about our services.*

You will notice I gave the executive a little more information than before, but not enough for him to make a judgment (or incorrect judgment) on the phone.

Objection No. 2:   *How do you do this?*

Response: *What we do is review your business plan with you after we sign a non-disclosure agreement, and then evaluate your needs as an executive to see how we can help you manage the business control ratchets. It will take about twenty minutes. Can we get together to chat? I will not waste your time.*

Again, a little more information, and then I close asking for the meeting.

NOTE: This particular company was selling professional services but the prospect could not tell by my sales value proposition exactly what I was selling because I focused on the results my service delivered and it interested him. When you look at business contracts for VC-funded companies, the ratchets and milestones were usually tied to having their services completed by a certain date. So, my sales value proposition actually matched my firm's services, but I had positioned us to appeal to the CEO and his business pain. By finding his pain, I bypassed the vice president of human resources and the vice president of operations who might normally deal with my firm for our services (and all of my competitors). By finding the CEO's pain, I became a doctor and was allowed to make a house call (the meeting).

Remember, it is not what type of product or service you sell that is important when selling to management; it is the results your product or service delivers to fix the senior executive's business pain that is important.

Objection No. 3: *Just send me some information. I'm busy.*

Response: *Yes, Mr. CEO, I know you are busy. But my firm specializes in working with CEOs like you and we personalize our programs and services, which is why I called. We don't have generic brochures, but instead we work with executives like you to fit your business needs by personalizing our offerings.*

Once we chat, I can then give you a more detailed overview of our offerings. It will only take twenty minutes and companies like Company X, Company Y, and Company Z were also busy, but after spending twenty minutes with us, they decided we could help. Would you like to get together early in the morning for breakfast (or a conference call)? I will not waste your time.

Objection No. 4: *I'm not interested.*

Response: Ask, **why**, then wait for an answer and respond, *I am surprised, Mr. CEO, since we have worked with other companies and CEOs like yourself including CEOs from Company X, Company Y, and Company Z and helped them with their needs. I would think that you would be open to new business concepts that would increase your corporate profits and increase your business value. Is it acceptable for me to send you some information and then follow up in a week or two to see if you may have reconsidered?*

If you get this response more than 50% of the time, then you need to review your sales value proposition.

The key of a sales value proposition is to intrigue the executive with an **unusual interest** in a concept they have not heard about before.

Be creative. Invent your SVP.

When I first started teaching this method, I had an experienced product sales manager ask me why I was not probing for the business opportunity on the first phone call to the management contact. My answer was that if you are going to call presidents and senior executives and actually engage them on the phone in a conversation, you cannot immediately start probing them like an inquisition on the first phone call.

That's how vendors act—and why most sales training methods fail. You end up insulting the prospect before you have earned the right to sell to them.

Do you honestly think you could cold call the vice president of a billon-dollar company or president of a family-owned business and talk to him for the first time on the telephone, start asking twenty probing questions on their current problems, and expect him to tell you what you need to know?

Of course not! All you are going to hear is click when they hang up the receiver.

You need to establish that you have the right to speak with them *first*, before the prospect will talk to you peer-to-peer. If your sales value proposition is crafted correctly, you will have greater access and success.

The goal of your telemarketing is to tease the prospect with the thought that your product or service can help them increase their business profit, reduce their expenses, or manage their consequences. Once they hear business value, more often than not, they will drop their guard and listen to your offering. Talk like a peer and act like a peer . . . and you will be treated like a peer.

You must put your business value up front when cold calling to sell more.

Review and Exercises

1. Schedule time in your appointment book to call three times each week. Load at least 300 companies into your database.

2. Develop a telemarketing script using the following steps:

   Step 1. Provide a personal introduction: *Hello, this is [YOUR NAME].*

   Step 2. Offer a professional courtesy: *Thank you for taking my call.*

   Step 3. Provide the sales value proposition: *We are [INSERT YOUR SALES VALUE PROPOSITION] specialists.*

   Step 4. Position that you are the right title level: *We work with [INSERT THEIR TITLE] like you.*

   Step 5. Describe the pain your sales value proposition fixes: *By using [YOUR SERVICE/PRODUCT], we can help you can increase revenue by eliminating/reducing [THEIR PAIN]*

Step 6.   Name drop references: *Companies like Company X, Company Y, and Company Z.*

Step 7.   Identify your company's name: *I am calling from [YOUR COMPANY]. (Optional – see notes provided.)*

Step 8.   Ask for a small amount of time: *Can we meet/chat for twenty minutes?*

Step 9.   Confirm that you value their time: *I will not waste your time.*

3. Develop talking points and responses to objections. Keep them handy.

4. Develop a voice-mail script.

Chapter 6

Meeting the Prospect for the First Time

After reading this chapter, you will know:

- What to expect during the first meeting

- What steps you should follow during the twenty-minute meeting

- How to develop talking points

- How to mine for opportunities

- How to move the first meeting into an executive briefing

It's not the pitch. It's the business pain you can fix!

What to Expect During the First Meeting

You have called the senior executive or small business president and now you have a twenty-minute meeting.

೮೪   ೮೪   ೮೪

Q: **Why twenty minutes?**

A: The key to dealing with executives is
       understanding they value their time more than
       you do. You are a salesperson. They get calls
       from people like you all of the time. To get the
       meeting, use your unique sales value
       proposition. It will make you the exception to
       the rule.

೮೪   ೮೪   ೮೪

By making the meeting for twenty minutes, you have
given the executive enough time to decide if you will
add value or waste their time. In twenty minutes,
either on the phone or in-person, a senior executive
can make a business decision to decide if you're a
business peer trying to help her or a vendor wasting
her time.

Your goals in your twenty-minute meeting are to:

- Reintroduce your sales value proposition
  position

- Validate you have the right to be speaking with
  them

- Mine for sales opportunities with the right questions

- Qualify senior executives to determine if they are in a transactional buying mode

- Make the executives take an action step with you during your sales cycle to prove they are qualified

- Set up another meeting to discuss buying, product, or service planning, or to have a discovery meeting

On your first meeting your goal is not to sell $50,000 worth of products or services. You are there to *prove you belong there*, mine for opportunities, and qualify the executive as an active buyer. If you try to sell at this early stage, you will not make it through the full twenty minutes because you will look like a vendor. Your sales value proposition is what got you in the door. Being able to stay is based on your preparation and skills as a salesperson.

Before we can discuss the twenty-minute meeting and its methodology, we must first discuss the selling process called *transactional sales*. Most salespeople are not familiar with this term. Instead, salespeople are familiar with *relationship* selling when selling to management. If you focus on establishing a sales relationship *before* the first sale, you are wasting your energy. I know, you may be saying, *No, this is wrong. I must have a relationship with the prospect for him to buy from me the first time.* That is incorrect. Management buys from vendors who help them increase income, decrease expenses, or manage risks. You don't have to have ten lunch meetings or four golf games to get a purchase order or contract. Those tactics work better when selling to lower management types. **With management, all you need is respect from the prospect.**

To sell to management, you must engage them like a consultant, strategist, or doctor—someone who is there to help—not like a vendor with an expense account.

- The definition of *relationship sales* is a "focus on generating revenue from clients who have long-term business needs."

- The definition of *transactional sales* is a "focus on generating revenue from prospects who have a business need now."

When you meet with management prospects in twenty-minute discovery meeting, you want to qualify them to see if they are transactional buyers or relationship buyers by having them answer specific transactional sales questions and asking them to take an action step with you during the sales cycle.

The key to selling more products and services to management is to focus on prospects who are in a transactional sales mode (regardless of how long your average sales cycle is). Additionally, you want to focus on prospects who take actions steps with you during the sales cycle so you will not waste your time with someone who is a professional looker, not a buyer.

The goal of your twenty-minute meeting is to qualify the prospect by having them take a sales action step in tandem with you. Qualified prospects that meet specific buying criteria are moved forward into an active sales model. Prospects who are not ready to buy or will not take action steps with you are moved into a passive sales model to be followed up with at a later time.

The twenty-minute meeting is broken down into **four steps**. Prepare for each step with talking points and use third-party research to show you are a specialist. Each step qualifies the prospect for buying capability and their transaction sales commitment. This meeting can be done in-person or over the phone, although in-person meetings are preferred.

Here are some guidelines to keep in mind:

▶ On your first meeting, come alone. Do not bring your direct sales manager. It is too early. Keep your sales management team invisible until a later date. If this is a major account, you (or your boss) might be tempted to bring in the heavy-hitting team to make the big pitch—but this is the wrong time to do it. Your first meeting is a peer-to-peer conversation between you and the management prospect. Prospects always defer to the highest title in the room, so if you bring your boss, the prospect will ignore you and just talk to your manager.

▶ Don't bring an overhead presentation. Management teams hate overhead presentations. Overhead presentations make you look like a vendor. Remember you are a peer.

▶ Do not bring multi-page company brochures. Management at the title of vice president and above do not read brochures, because they don't have time. They read single fact sheets and white papers.

Steps of the First Meeting

Step 1: The Introduction. (Length: two to five minutes) Discuss your firm's history, your client base, and your sales value proposition (SVP).

> *Mr./Ms. Prospect, thank you for meeting with me. As discussed in our call, my firm, [INSERT YOUR COMPANY NAME], specializes in [INSERT YOUR VALUE]. We started operations in [INSERT YEAR] and have consulted with over hundreds of companies worldwide on their corporate sales and marketing programs. Our clients include a broad range of companies, both public and private, small and large, and include Company X, Company Y and Company Z and we specifically work with CEOs, vice presidents of sales, managing directors, and vice presidents of marketing only.*

Do not overwhelm your prospect during the introduction stage about who you are and how great your company is. There will be plenty of time later to manage the flow of this information as needed.

Step 2: The Bridge. (Length: five minutes) Discuss industry business pains that relate to your prospect's market. This stage allows you to demonstrate to the prospect you are an industry knowledge specialist. Quote five to seven third-party industry research studies (from consulting companies or industry magazines) about current business problems. **Never quote your firm as an "expert" or "research authority."** If the management prospect in the room disagrees with your observations, they will have an issue with you. Instead, by quoting third-party industry research, if they disagree with your comments, their comments are aimed at someone who is not present.

The reason this step is called the *bridge* is because it migrates (or bridges) you to the next step, where you will start probing the prospect on his business needs, his business pains, and the qualifications to buy.

> *Mr./Ms. Prospect, since our firm specializes in [INSERT YOUR VALUE] we constantly monitor the best practices of the pharmaceutical (or healthcare, insurance, logistics, hospitality, manufacturing, etc.) industry. Recently, ABC Magazine said there are five main business* **events** *currently affecting the pharmaceutical market and their sales teams. These include sales staff not trained to sell to management, the average sales cycle is increasing, gross margin per sales are shrinking, account salespeople turnover is increasing, and marketing costs per sales have increased 10%.*

Never use the words *business problems* or *business pain* with a prospect. If the senior executive's ego is floating around the room during your sales call, he will not admit that he has business problems. Instead, substitute the word *problems* with the word *events*. When researching your five to seven business industry issues, try to find events that correspond to the business results your product or service will deliver. Always quote your research source during this step.

Step 3: Probing and Transactional Questioning. (Length: five to ten minutes) During this stage, you want to confirm that the prospect is a qualified buyer, he is in a transactional mode of buying, and he has business problems (events) your product or service can fix. To bridge the transition between Step 2 to Step 3 say,

> *Mr./Ms. Prospect, as discussed, the [INSERT YOUR INDUSTRY] industry is currently experiencing multiple business events, and I was wondering if you have any of these events occurring in your firm?*

Now, based on how the prospect answers your question, you will have two paths to take during the sales process.

▶ **Option A:** If the prospect says, *yes*, and names one of the business events that is affecting their industry and their company, then focus on this issue and how your product or service can help them. To move your prospect forward through the sales cycle, make sure you ask the following qualifying questions directly or indirectly in a conversational mode.

- *Do you have a budget? If so, how much funding have you allocated?*

- *Who is making the decision to buy?*

- *Who is signing the purchase order and/or contract?*

- *Who else will be involved in this decision besides yourself?*

- *What are the business consequences if you do not fix these business events?*

- *How is this business decision being made (committee, RFP, etc.)?*

- *When do you want our product or service operational (installed, bought, launched, in inventory, etc.)?*

I am always amazed how many experienced salespeople don't ask these questions during the beginning of their sales cycle. I don't know if salespeople fear the answers, simply project their needs onto the prospect, or assume the manager is a qualified buyer, but more often than not, many salespeople do not ask these direct questions early enough in the sales cycle. The value of selling to management is that they are usually more honest and informative in their answers. Thus, don't hesitate. Be *professionally blunt* and ask direct questions.

Step 3 in the twenty-minute meeting is the checkpoint where you decide whether this prospect is a qualified buyer or a professional looker. If the prospect answers these questions positively and they appear to be a qualified buyer, **then you should proceed to Step 4.**

▶ **Option B: If the prospect says,** *My company is a well-run operation and we do not have any of our industry's business problems,* then the manager's ego is floating around the room with you. Why? Statistically, their company should have at least one of the industry's top business issues if you have done your industry research for Step 2.

When you hear this response, reply with questions that lead with one of the following words, *how, why, how long, when,* or *what.* Respond to the prospect by saying, *Mr. Prospect, I'm surprised. . .*

- *How come your firm is not experiencing any of these business events which are common in our industry?*

- *Why does your firm not have these business events (business pains)?*

- *How long ago did you think about using this project (inventory, service)?*

- *When will you review this area again?*

- *What is the reason for your firm not having these events?*

The goal in Step 3 is to get the executive to confirm they have a business pain that you can fix and they are in a transactional sales cycle (buying mode). At this point, many salespeople believe if the prospect does not identify a business pain their product or service can fix, they can *convince* them to buy with their superior selling skills. This is a mistaken belief of inexperienced salespeople.

Management will buy when you can help them fix their business pains. Yes, you can wear prospects down over time to sell them something, but all this will do is waste valuable selling time you would have otherwise spent with prospects who are ready to buy. Prospects who are not ready to buy (during whatever your average sales cycle length is) should be put into a passive marketing mode and followed up on a monthly basis. It is not productive for you to project your needs to sell to prospects who are not ready.

If, after spending fifteen minutes with the prospect, you find they are not qualified, nor can they direct you to someone who is qualified, then put them into a passive marketing mode, follow up with them monthly, and get out of Dodge. Why? Because you must focus on buyers, not professional lookers.

Step 4: First Meeting Completion. (Length: two to five minutes) If you have reached Step 4, you are now sitting with a prospect who is a transactional buyer based on the previous questions and the prospect's answers. During Step 4, you want to discuss with the prospect how your product or service can help fix their current business event, and that you are a specialist who helps management executives like them increase income, decrease expenses (either in their department or the company as a whole), or manage risks through the purchase of your product or service. The goal of Step 4 is to set up a new meeting (discovery meeting, executive briefing, project scoping meeting, presentation, etc.) **that will last approximately one hour in length**.

Why only one hour?

Remember, selling to management is done through a sequential sales process. Jumping steps does not accelerate your sales cycle. In fact, it slows it down. At this stage of your sales process, you do not want to camp out in the senior executive's office for four hours demonstrating how great you are—because they are not ready for this overproduction yet.

As in previous sales steps, before you spend excessive time with an executive (an hour or more), you are going to re-qualify them again as a buyer instead of a professional looker.

Do not set up a discovery meeting with management unless you know and understand the prospect's answers to the questions you asked in Step 3. The prospect's responses to your questions will help you decide if this is a qualified buyer or a professional looker and what action steps are needed on your part to move this prospect forward in the sales cycle.

The total time for your first meeting with the prospect should be no more than twenty minutes.

Talking Points for Prospect Meetings

The sales process, by its very nature, requires repetitive tasks. Cold calling, sending out follow-up e-mails to prospects, developing proposals, and managing customer issues are all daily tasks required to hit and exceed your sales quota.

In consulting with many companies, it surprises me how often experienced salespeople do not plan their sales calls and fall into a repetitive presentation model based on previous experiences with "like" prospects. They just wing it because they are *senior* salespeople. **Do not autosell. Always prepare for each new twenty-minute meeting like it is your first sales opportunity.**

Before meeting the client, you should have reviewed their web site (if they have one), their annual report (if they are public), and any other business information you can gather. Professional salespeople do not shoot from the hip. The key to supporting your sales value proposition is preparation.

From this information, you are going to compile **talking points** for you. Your talking points should list potential pain opportunities your firm can fix based on what you sell, and your goals for the twenty-minute meeting.

Do not wing this part. Type out your talking points. You will be tempted not to do this, but if you type the talking points, you will script your dialogue and goals and help your team understand the business issues you must discuss. *Carry them with you and review them as you chat with the senior executive.* It will help you stay focused on your topics and meeting goals.

When holding your first twenty-minute meeting with a prospect on the phone or in-person always prepare specific talking points to manage your conversation (and any sales team member who is with you). Your talking points should include:

- Issues you want to communicate during the meeting

- Points you want your sales team members to avoid discussing

- The goal for the sales meeting

- The questions or sales objections you anticipate the prospect will ask or discuss

- The questions or topics each team member will be responsible for answering

On the next page, I've provided a **First Meeting Talking Points** form. In Appendix C, you will find a blank form that you can copy and adapt to your needs.

First Meeting Talking Points

Date Prepared:	7/12/04
Sales Rep:	Shelly Smith
Client's Name:	ABC Physician Facility
Contacts:	Rick Jones, CEO and Mary Mays, COS
Business Type:	Physician facilities targeting specialty practices.
Public/Private:	Private
# of Employees:	47
Business URL:	www.abchospitalfacility.com
Industry Business Pains:	Patient management; need to reduce their advertising expenses and increase revenue through alternative means.
Industry Terminology:	Board Certified, Clinical Research, Revenue Replacement Model, Human Capital Costs
Sales value proposition to communicate:	*We are Profit Improvement Specialists for physicians and specialty practices.* We help medical facilities automate their patient management, and increase the effectiveness of their advertising and marketing. • We offer the ability to automate patient management. • We use e-Zine newsletters for channel distribution. • We work with senior executives only.
Our Associates Talking Points:	Dan Kelley • On-line development process and opt-in e-mail usage • Executive briefing meeting
Areas to Avoid:	Had bad experience with direct mail; does not want to use third-party subcontractors
Meeting Goals:	Set up new 1-hour meeting; Budget; Time frame; Competition; Who is making the decision
Goal Time Period:	One Week
Potential Purchase:	Patient management software, e-Zine newsletter; consulting, opt-in e-mail
Value of Deal:	$50,000 this year
Additional Comments	The client is anxious to buy based on need to expand. He is not price resistant, but seeks value.

Figure 3.   *First Meeting Talking Points form.* As part of your Value Forward Tool Box, you should complete this form and hand it to each of your team members prior to the twenty-minute executive meeting.

Managing the First Meeting

In a premeditated selling process, it's important you try to manage the sales cycle instead of having the prospect manage you. At times, this is not always possible. Here is a business tool you can use to try to maintain control.

It is called a *client engagement outline*. A client engagement outline lists the **sales steps you expect buyers to take as you lead them through your selling process** and communicate immediately how you expect the sales cycle to proceed. After the first twenty-minute meeting, if a prospect is a qualified buyer, hand them the outline (see Figure 4) and say:

> *Mr./Ms. Prospect, based on our firm's strength as specialists in [INSERT YOUR SALES VALUE PROPOSITION], we have found this engagement process helps us help you determine if our product (or service) is the right fit for you based on your business needs.*

Following is a detailed engagement process of discovery, presentation, and discussion to help prospective clients experience the value of your product, service, or program. This approach helps both you and your prospect identify and fit the strategic and tactical requirements needed for a business relationship.

Client Engagement Outline	
Phase 1	Information Exchange
Phase 2	Executive Briefing—Business Needs Assessment
Phase 3	Executive Briefing—Business Discovery
Phase 4	Service or Product Presentation
Phase 5	Prospect Proposal Development
Phase 6	Executive Briefing—Proposal Delivery and Discussion
Phase 7	[YOUR COMPANY] Selected as a Preferred Vendor
Phase 8	Executive Briefing—Proposal and Contract Finalized
Phase 9	[YOUR COMPANY] Assigns Team Leader to Manage Product/ Service Delivery

Figure 4. *Client Engagement Outline.* A list of steps expected during the sales cycle.

This tool allows you to lay out the interaction you need in order to sell to management as a peer. It also prepares the prospect for what is required of them during each sales step. Always use an engagement outline at the beginning of your sales cycle to manage your prospect's buying pattern. To create an engagement outline, break down your current sales cycle into individual sales steps.

Mining for Opportunities

The best method for selling products or services to management executives and presidents of small companies is mining for business opportunities at your first twenty-minute meeting. Remember, you are not there to sell, but instead to validate your position as a specialist and to confirm you are qualified to speak with the executive. Additionally, you are there to prove you will not waste their time. Your sales value proposition got you there. Now, you need to develop an interactive conversation with the executive to identify and mine for opportunities.

Many sales training courses talk about asking open-ended questions to flush out a prospect's true needs and wants. **Forget it.** Those sales approaches are **old school** and are designed for middle- or lower-management who have a tendency not to know all of the facts, or who play games. You are now dealing with an executive, and that system does not work. You are behaving like a peer. Do not waste her time. Lean forward across her desk, look her in the eye, and ask **DIRECT** questions.

When working with executives, always ask direct questions. Asking direct questions of management is being *professionally* blunt. If they see you as a peer, then you have the right to speak like a peer. To do this, you need the following tools to be successful:

1. Gather **factual industry information about the business the client is involved in**. If they are a hotel company or an insurance company

or a local car dealership, you need to know some basic facts about that market segment.

2. With this information in hand, you need to **deploy industry comments and vernacular during the first five minutes of your meeting**. This allows you to validate your position and to reinforce your sales value proposition as a specialist.

3. Once you have explained your sales value proposition and discussed the industry as a whole, you then need to **tie your sales value proposition to the industry and discuss how you can help solve business problems for the executive**. Be a doctor and relieve the pain.

The following are actual case histories of this program being presented to senior executives.

Case Study—Meeting the Prospect: Relieving the Pain (Gaming Industry)

In one case, I communicated the following:

> *Mr. President, as discussed on the phone, we are **Specialists in Casino Player Retention**. We accomplish this by working with the property's management team to analyze player retention and then develop methodologies and services to increase management controls of that revenue stream. We know the gaming industry is currently going through a difficult time with customer retention due to the diversification of gaming throughout the U.S. and there is an increased demand to generate more gaming dollars per player.*

By using this model, you will be able bridge your introduction, your validation, and the communication of your sales value proposition to the questioning (mining) of opportunities.

Once you have stated the above bridge, you will probably hear a question like, *How do you accomplish casino player retention?*

My response was, *We do this through an organized process where we analyze the casino's systems to determine their effectiveness on player retention and their effect on revenue. Mr. VP, how is your firm handling this industry issue?*

What have I done?

Instead of selling features and benefits (like many salespeople do), I have focused on the industry pain and then transferred that pain to the management executive in terms of revenue and expenses. Using the feature and benefit sales method of your product and/or professional services will never capture the attention that focusing on the client's pain will.

When I transferred the industry pain to the executive, I never directly said he had the same industry problems, but you can assume that he would not have asked to meet me if he was not concerned about the same issues, as well as intrigued by my sales value proposition.

By discussing the industry pains, it allowed the executive to keep face and opened up the door for him to respond about his firm's individual needs (pain). By continuing to turn the pain into **income** and **expense issues,** I maintained my legitimate right to be talking to the senior decision maker.

Be the pain management doctor and earn the right to be a peer!

If you can find the pain, you can be a doctor and fix it. When a person is injured in a car accident, they never ask, *How much will it cost to get well?* Instead, the first thing they say is, *Get me the best doctor and take away the pain!*

Case Study—Meeting the Prospect: Relieving the Pain (Auto Industry)

In another case, I communicated the following:

Mr. VP, as indicated when you and I spoke on the phone, we specialize in profit improvement for the auto dealership industry. We do this by helping senior executives like you automate their communication to their client base. We accomplish this through a premeditated briefing program where we analyze your business needs and then generate an assessment to help your firm increase top-line revenue. The auto industry is moving from a decentralized distribution channel to a centralized channel, making it more difficult for mega dealers like yourself to maintain connectivity to your paying customers on a localized basis.

What have I done?

1. I reconfirmed my sales value proposition.

2. I established that we are knowledgeable about the auto industry.

3. I connected the client's pain to my sales value proposition.

Fortune 1000 Companies. One way to successfully sell products and professional services to Fortune 1000 clients faster is to bring a company operations specialist or strategist with you at the first twenty-minute meeting. Why? Instead of waiting until the second or third meeting, like some people do, you can pre-qualify the opportunities discussed and quickly establish your firm as a specialist with a strategist present who can discuss client case studies from the participant's point of view instead of a salesperson's.

As stated earlier, it is important for you to not bring your sales manager on the first meeting. As mentioned before, the reason for this is that the prospect will defer to the sales manager and you will lose control of communication with the prospect.

If you follow the methods provided in this course, have done your research on the client, and have scheduled your meeting with a VP or above, you will not be wasting the strategist's time. Large sales organizations will normally balk at this process, saying it is too expensive to have a billable operations or product person on the first call, but this method will accelerate the sales cycle for all Fortune 1000 opportunities, so a defensible ROI is there.

Mining Questions That Work. You've had your prospect in an interactive discussion and there is mutual agreement that the prospect's industry has pain. After probing, the client begins to express his firm's own pain. To continue the dialogue, try these pain-probing questions:

1. *How does the board of directors see this industry event (name the issue or pain)?*

2. *Has your firm attempted to respond to this industry issue?*

3. *How have they responded?*

4. *What is your firm's direction/timeline this calendar year to resolve this industry problem?*

5. *How would the elimination or reduction of this event help your corporate goals this year?*

6. *You mentioned your firm was experiencing other events as well. Could you explain? How have these areas affected your business?*

7. *Have those events disrupted corporate profitability?*

8. *Has this area disrupted corporate expense management?*

Remember, Value Forward Selling techniques focus on three areas to be successful for management executives and presidents of small companies: **revenue, expenses, and risk management.**

► If you are selling wholesale jewelry to a retail chain, ask yourself, *how will my inventory increase revenue, decrease expenses, or manage risks* (more inventory turn, greater margin contributions, etc.)?

► If you are selling an automation product, evaluate how the prospect will use it to increase corporate revenue or decrease expenses.

► If you are selling professional services to a thirty-person company, create a model that demonstrates how your service will increase revenue, decrease expenses, or manage risks.

If you talk about other areas, you will never be successful selling products and services in volume. When management executives and presidents make decisions on purchases, **it always comes back to revenue, expenses, and consequence management**. Focus on these areas and watch your commissions increase. Many salespeople focus too much on product features and service benefits, adversely affecting their closing ratio.

Focus on the clients' pain. Then, turn your product or service into doctor's medicine that will fix this pain with either an increase in sales, reduction in expenses, or management of risks.

Your Twenty Minutes Are Up

As you hit the self-imposed twenty-minute time barrier, keep talking if the executive is asking you questions about your service or products. It is their time, and you are there to develop a peer-to-peer respect, but after thirty minutes, you should wrap up and recap in quick detail the pains that the executive has identified as existing in his firm.

Look the executive in the eye and say:

> *Mr./Ms. Executive, I appreciate the time you
> have spent with me. Based on my commitment to
> take no more than twenty minutes of your time,
> what I would like to do is set up a new meeting
> for our management teams to discuss in more
> detail how we can increase your business revenue
> (or decrease expenses) using our programs. We
> usually do this in an executive briefing format
> with you and your management team. It will
> only take one hour. When would be a good day?*

If you have positioned your sales value proposition
correctly, he will set up a meeting. If the executive
hesitates, wait for his response. If the executive says
they are not really interested at this time, **ask why**. If
he discussed pain management with you, there should
not be any logical reason for him to not see you again.

Once you hear his objection, focus on the pain and
then communicate again your firm's process to
eliminate it. Act surprised that he would not want to
explore more detailed methods to increase revenue,
reduce expenses, or manage risks with you at another
meeting. **Again, ask for the second meeting and
tell the executive you will not waste their time.**

Studies consistently show that salespeople who
continually ask for meetings from qualified prospects,
get them. Ask the executive at least *three* times for the

next meeting, slightly changing your request method each time. Remember, if you have done your homework and they are qualified, you are sitting in front of a decision maker who has a pain that needs to be fixed.

The first meeting with the management executive or the president of a small company should always involve a *conceptual business discussion*. The second meeting is your discovery or executive briefing meeting to fine tune your offering to the prospect's needs.

Remember, to get your second meeting, you must use buyer words, not vendor words.

Wrong Verbiage	**Right Verbiage**
We sell web sites.	We work with clients like you to increase digital revenue through automation.
We offer accounting consulting.	We help CFOs reduce human capital costs.
We offer custom jewelry at low pricing.	Our programs increase your revenue per square foot and reduce returns.

When there are more than two sales opportunities,
write down the project types that are available and
then ask again for a one-hour meeting with the
executive team to discuss one of those projects. If
there is more than one project, service, or product that
your firm can sell the prospect, set up **separate**
meetings for each. *Do not bunch these subjects together or
you risk losing all of them at once.*

If the executive says, *Your [SALES VALUE
PROPOSITION] process sounds interesting. Talk to my secretary
and have her set up a meeting with my VPs and me,* as you
leave the senior executive's office, say hello to the
secretary and inform her that her boss said she needs
to set up a meeting for him and you in the near future.
Then ask her (right there while you're standing in front
of her) if she would check his schedule to see when he
would be available next.

If the executive says, *This is interesting. I want you to meet
with John, my Vice President of Delivery,* ask the senior
management executive (while you are sitting in his
office), would he e-mail John to let him know he
would like you two to meet.

If the executive doesn't walk you out to the main
door, call John immediately from the lobby and say,
*Hi John, my name is [YOUR NAME] and I just met with
[MANAGEMENT EXECUTIVE'S NAME]. We specialize in*

[SALES VALUE PROPOSITION] and [EXECUTIVE'S NAME] wanted you and I to meet.

If, after you offer the executive your sales value proposition and the pitch about increasing company revenue and reducing expenses, he still says, *I am not the right person,* then ask, *Could you direct me to the right person in the company you want me to speak to?* Then call those contacts and tell them the senior executive asked you to call, and start the process all over again.

> ಛ   ಛ   ಛ

Q: **Why does this selling process work?**

A: Today's economy is dragging businesses through a business paradigm shift. The only way management will invest in anything is if it directly or indirectly increases income, decreases expenses, or manages risks. Remember, it's not a cost issue. It's a business value issue.

> ಛ   ಛ   ಛ

In a complex business world, senior executives do not need another generalist. **What they seek are companies who are specialists and can help them fix their pain. They seek doctors or pain management specialists.**

The words used in this script are specific to these needs. When communicating how you differ from your competitors through your sales value proposition and marketing materials, focus on these management pressure points:

- Increase corporate profits

- Reduce corporate expenses

- Manage business consequences

- Integrate business department communication

- Become a specialist in

    o Performance Management

    o Customer Retention

    o Customer Maintenance

    o Customer Capture

    o Client Communication

Case Study—Meeting the Prospect: The First Time

Using the previous method, I penetrated one of the largest hotels companies in the world. For two years, our company had been unable to successfully sell professional services to this client in volume. I was asked to help.

Here is what happened:

1. I cold called the vice president and sent him a business book.

---

2. I spoke with him on the phone and explained to him our unique sales value proposition and that we were specialists.

3. He said he was interested, but he was traveling for the next thirty days to hotel sites. He then directed me to call another vice president and set up a meeting.

4. I called the vice president and told him his business peer requested I meet with him. I also told him I would like to meet for twenty minutes, and I would not waste his time.

5. I sent him a book, a one-page description of my marketing sales value proposition, and met with him in his private office.

6. I introduced myself again, stated our sales value proposition, explored the industry pains, discussed why we were different, how we could fix those pains, and then mined for opportunities.

The meeting outcome:

The twenty-minute meeting was successful and lasted longer than anticipated. When I left, there were three other vendors waiting in the vice president's office for their late meetings. I left with three new separately scheduled one-hour meetings (all of which I had scheduled while I sat in the executive's office) to discuss three business pains the firm was experiencing.

Within six months, we became a preferred vendor with the client and were scheduled to generate in excess of $10,000,000 in business over the next three years.

By developing a sales value proposition that appealed to management and discussing profit improvement and expense reduction, I was able to sell more conceptually and get the business. **I became a peer.**

Management buys by impression; supervisors buy by price, feature, function, or service descriptions.

Review and Exercises

1. Take the First Meeting Talking Points form and complete it based on a prospect you would like to sell to. This will help you build a thinking process as you set up meetings with the prospect.

2. Make a list of mining questions that you may use in a first meeting. If you sell to several verticals, develop a list of questions for each vertical industry.

Chapter 6
Meeting the Prospect for the First Time

Chapter 7

Presenting to Prospects - The Executive Briefing

After reading this chapter, you will know:

- What to expect during executive briefings and discovery meetings

- How to give a whiteboard presentation

- How to prepare yourself and your team for the presentation

- When to use slide presentations with management prospects

- When to use portfolio presentations

What to Expect During the Executive Briefings/Discovery Meetings

Based on the hundreds of companies and sales teams we have worked with, I believe that half of all deals are won or loss based on the execution of the presentation in the executive meeting. Why? The executive presentation is the one opportunity you have to capture the mindsets of the management team and their subordinates—in the same room at one time—to communicate your firm's specializations and specific business value, and control their perception of why they should buy from you.

After the presentation is completed, management teams and their subordinates return to their individual suites, office cubes, and steering committees to regroup later and make a decision on your business offering. Once they disperse, their accessibility as a whole diminishes.

A polished executive presentation is like crowd control. Your goal is to imprint a *visual brochure* in everyone's minds—an impression of why they should buy from you.

Your success in the executive presentation needs to be centered on capturing your audience's mindset in a unique way so they easily remember your firm instead of your competition. Additionally, your goal is for your prospects to see you as a specialist instead of a generalist.

When making a group presentation, it is important to realize that every person invited to the presentation has a reason to be there. Collect their business cards at the beginning of the presentation so you can refer to them when addressing each person. Do not minimize the title of any person. You are seeking acceptance by the group as a whole about your sales value proposition. There is a tendency (even by very experienced salespeople) to ignore lower-titled attendees and play to the senior title in the room (many times your management contact). Doing this is a strategic mistake. This *faux pas* causes many salespeople to lose deals.

Under Value Forward Selling, you actively seek out management to launch the sales cycle. But, when presenting to a group of people who have been instructed to be there by your management contact, make sure everyone is treated equally. A person with a manager or director title may not make the decision, but when the steering committee regroups to make a decision, that person could sink you as a decision influencer, just because you hurt their ego by ignoring them.

Running a presentation or holding an executive briefing is like being on Broadway. You have to grab the audience's full attention to demonstrate your sales value proposition and distinguish yourself from all other competitors.

NOTE: **Never let attendees see you sweat**. If something goes wrong during a service discussion or product presentation, just keep moving. In many cases, clients will not even notice in a high-level presentation.

Remember, 50% of sales decisions are based on the quality of the presentation.

As the presentation unfolds, ask questions of the group as a whole and individuals specifically. When you ask questions directed to a specific person, use the attendee's first name (remember you collected their business cards at the beginning of the meeting). The key to getting answers from decision makers is to keep asking questions. If you continually ask **why** and **how**, you will be more successful.

Executive: *We need to automate our HR system.*
Salesperson: *Why? How quickly will you make that decision?*

Executive: *We are thinking about staying with our current vendor.*
Salesperson: *Why?*
How has that current vendor performed for you?

Executive: *Our CEO wants us to focus on a redesign of our shipping department.*
Salesperson: *Why? How will you make a vendor selection?*

Executive: *We are considering installing a new CRM system.*

Salesperson: *Why? How can we help you install that CRM system?*

Small Businesses. In small company sales, this is even more effective, but potentially dangerous. Many of the attendees in the presentation may be related, so always respect everyone in the room. Ask *why* and *how* cautiously.

Giving Whiteboard Presentations

Most senior executives have seen enough slide presentations to last two lifetimes. Due to the over proliferation of this communication method, good presenters are reverting **BACK** to the whiteboard.

New studies from professional training associations indicate that a slick overhead and whiteboard presentation gets better retention and a higher approval rating than a slide show presentation. To energize your client presentation (even if you are demonstrating technology), cut back on the computer-aided presentation and start interacting in a demonstrative way using a whiteboard (provided there is one in the room you are meeting in).

The whiteboard presentation works extremely well when you are competing against large, established, competitive players. Their presentations are usually *too slick, rigid,* and *slide-show driven* for most management.

Again, *do not wing this part of the presentation.* Think it through, plan, develop a process, and practice it. The best method for this kind of presentation is a process I developed almost twenty years ago called the **Three Box Monty™**. The Three Box Monty uses an educational process called *experiential learning.* Experiential learning occurs when the listener (your prospect) "experiences" your business value while using interaction as a communication process. The Three Box Monty™ presentation method uses multi-sensory tools to make your message and business value stand out.

The Three Box Monty™ was not developed to educate future salespeople, but instead as a way for a quota-carrying salesperson to distinguish him/herself against large established Fortune 1000 competitors when presenting to management.

Years ago, like today, most people trooped into the conference room, pulled out their marketing materials, cranked up the overhead projector, and started describing to the key executives the features and functions of their products and services. After three or four vendor presentations in a row, everyone starts looking like vanilla ice cream to the executive management team, making it difficult for them to distinguish you from your competitors. So, based on these experiences, I developed the Three Box Monty™.

I have used this method and taught it to thousands of salespeople—it works. It uses psychology, strategy, experiential sales techniques, speaking techniques, and communication methods that enable prospects to create a visual brochure of why you are different. But before I discuss the Three Box Monty™ format in detail, let's first review some preliminary points for your executive presentation.

Preparing for Your Executive Briefing

One area where many experienced salespeople fail is in the preparation of a sales call. Always prepare typed talking points for your presentation.

Case Study—Presenting to Prospects: A Presentation Without Talking Points

I remember early in my career accompanying the vice president of sales and three development and operations types to present to a Fortune 50 company.

When I asked if we were going to have a pre-meeting to prepare for our product demonstration, the vice president of sales said that he had been working with the prospect for over a year and he was ready. Additionally, he said I should just listen and learn.

We all trooped over to the prospect's conference room, took our seats, and waited for the meeting to begin. The vice president of sales set up his overhead projector for our product demonstration and waited for the executives to arrive.

As soon as the introductions were made, the vice president started into his sales pitch and didn't stop talking for forty-five minutes. Moving from the slide presentation to a products demo, he seemed smooth and knowledgeable.

After forty-five minutes, the clients started to ask questions that the vice president responded to firmly and in detail. After an hour and a half, the vice president of sales had completed his demonstration and asked if there were any additional questions.

The prospect's vice president of operations, who had sat through the entire demonstration quietly said *no* and thanked us very much for our time. When the vice president asked what would be the next step, we were informed that the Fortune 50 management team would get back to us.

So, we packed up our bags and headed out to our rental car, threw our bags into the trunk, and raced to the airport to catch our flight home. As we headed down the highway at ninety miles an hour, the vice president of sales (now regarded as Captain Smooth by our sales team) said loudly in the backseat, *How do you guys think it went? They seem pretty interested!*

Well, they weren't. Thirty days later we were told the Fortune 50 company had signed a Letter of Intent with one of our competitors and they were currently working out the details of the contract—a contract worth $13 million!

Throughout my career I have seen this scenario over and over again. It is hard to believe, but experienced sales executives and management teams continually wing it when they are on a sales call. Salespeople spend a large amount of time prospecting, marketing, and positioning their company to meet and greet the right decision makers, but then fail to prep for the big meeting. **<u>Successful salespeople do not wing it.</u>**

Case Study—Presenting to Prospects: A Second Meeting Gone Wrong

In one meeting, I sat as an observer with several vice presidents of a Fortune 1000 company, along with the vendor VP and his presentation team. The vendor had been in business for multiple years and had an unusual product that this Fortune 1000 company could use immediately. The vendor VP had over ten years of experience in sales and had been previously employed by one of the largest companies in the world.

Prior to this current position, the vendor VP had been exposed to multiple structured sales training courses on how to sell. Yet, as I observed his presentation, it was *amateur hour at the comedy club.*

At the beginning of the meeting, the management prospect informed everyone that he had only one hour available for this presentation. So to hit the timeline, the vendor VP immediately launched into his presentation without supplying any company history or sales value proposition.

Mistake 1:   ***Don't make the prospect wonder who you are.***

Mistake 2:   ***Always provide an intriguing reason to draw the prospect into the presentation.***

As the prospect VPs started to ask questions about the vendor's history, another presenter in the room attempted to respond and was cut off by the vendor VP, who bellowed that he would answer that question.

Mistake 3:   ***Always work as a team.***

I could feel the tension in the room between the vendor and the prospects. Unfortunately, it got worse. During the product presentation, the vendor VP's demonstration failed. He then started talking out loud, *Something is wrong here, it's not working right.*

Mistake 4:   ***Never let them see you sweat.***

To prevent this type of embarrassment, follow the steps provided in this sales course and be a sales professional. Always prepare talking points and discussion topics for yourself and everyone involved.

Building Your Talking Points Script

The day has arrived. You cold called the management executive with your **sales value proposition,** and convinced him you are a specialist. You held a twenty-minute mining conversation, confirmed they are a qualified buyer, and have been given a one-hour executive presentation meeting to "walk and talk" what you do in detail. You are up to bat. What do you do?

If you are using team selling, the first thing to do is to get everyone together who is involved in the meeting and chat about the format, the client, and the presentation pain concept. Again, the key to Value Forward Selling is always being prepared.

I cannot tell you how many times I have sat with a client's experienced sales team and watched them fumble and wing it through their presentation. Decide today that you will never wing a presentation and you will always be a pro. Follow these guidelines and you will be more successful.

1. You are the salesperson. Your commission is riding on this presentation. You are responsible for how the meeting goes and for what people say or don't say while your client and their management team is in the presentation room. **THIS IS YOUR SHOW**. You need to tell

everyone who is on your presenting team how the process is going to evolve. **DO NOT** let an operations person, a business architect, or your boss dictate how the meeting's agenda will develop or how the presentation will go. *It is your commission.* Control them and don't let them wing it. If you lose the deal (and your commission) because your boss said the wrong thing in your executive briefing, your boss will still hold you responsible for losing the deal.

2. Create an internal agenda for your team that dictates who will speak on what subjects and what topics they should not talk about. List their names next to the subject matter and time sequence on your **Talking Points Script.**

3. Allocate a maximum time for each subject and speaker to talk about during your presentation.

4. Accept that as the salesperson, you *should not* do most of the talking.

5. Review with the group the slide presentation you will use, if any. Provide a hard copy of the presentation and the agenda in a folder to each member of the team. Include contact names, telephone numbers, time of the meeting, and the street directions.

6. Make sure you list a participant's name next to each presentation slide, so that everyone knows the topics he/she is responsible for and must be able to speak about.

7. In your Talking Points document, list who will answer the client's questions on each specific subject. Generally, if there is a technical question, the salesperson should be quiet (even if they know the answer) and let the technical people respond.

8. Create a *Top Twenty Tough Questions Clients May Ask* document with sales and technical responses typed up and handed out to all presenters at your pre-meeting. Be prepared to answer these questions. **Make sure you are prepared for the questions you fear most.**

9. Generally, the salesperson handles presenter introductions, the company overview, the sales value proposition, the industry pains, the pains expressed by the senior executive, requests for pricing, and the wrap-up.

10. The operations and engineering team members are responsible for technical, production, and functional descriptions of your products and services; product skill set reviews; services; and delivery time schedules.

11. Create three typed questions, to engage the personalities and egos in the room, for each manager or listener from your company who will attend the executive briefing. If you are getting help with the executive briefing, distribute these questions to your team to ask their counterpart in the meeting (i.e., have your operations person ask the prospect's operation manager questions; have your finance person ask questions of the financial buyer).

12. Create a one-page blank sheet of paper with your company name on the top, your sales value proposition underneath it and three square boxes on the page, set up as shown (see Figure 5 on the following page).

13. Your team members will feel pressure to contribute at your presentation. However, the goal of your executive briefing is to win business, not make your team members feel warm and fuzzy. Control your team's communication correctly and you will prevent the wrong message or response from being said and you will win more business.

In your pre-meeting preparation, teach your team members to *never say no* in a client meeting. Teach them to say, *That's a possibility. Can we get back to you on it?* **The rule of thumb is if you say no three times or more**

in an executive briefing, the prospect will only remember what you *cannot* do, rather than what you *can* do. By their very nature, operational, technical, and support staff who attend executive briefings are conservative and never want to try anything new. All custom requests have a price, so let management make that decision, not an operations person sitting in your meeting who is worried that he is already too busy. **Be a sales-driven company, not a product- or service-driven company.**

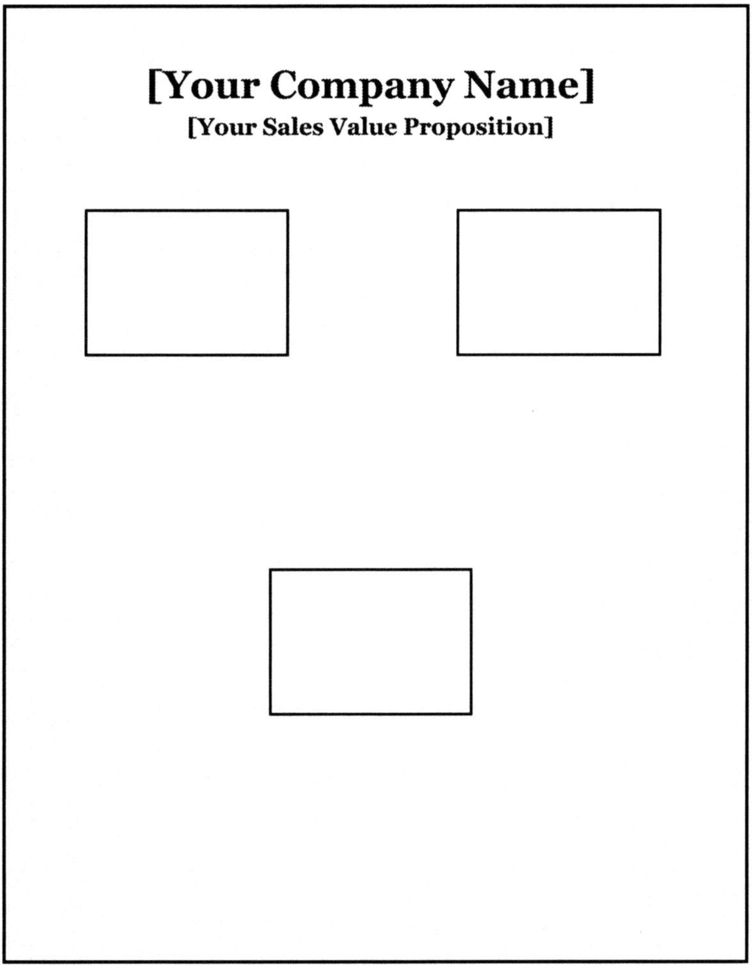

[Your Company Name]
[Your Sales Value Proposition]

Figure 5.   *Three Box Monty form.* As part of your Value
Forward Tool Box, this is a blank document that is
handed to each attendee at the one-hour meeting.

Presentation Talking Points

Lead Presenter's Name (salesperson):_____
Client's name_____
Client's URL_____
Client's Address/Briefing Location_____

Briefing Date_____Briefing Time_____
Time Allocated to Briefing by Client_____

Meeting Lead Attendee:
Name_____ Title_____Telephone_____

Meeting Attendees:
Name_____ Title_____Telephone_____
Name_____ Title_____Telephone_____
Name_____ Title_____Telephone_____

Client's Pain Issues_____

Product or Service To Be Presented_____

Presenter's Name_____
Title_____
Responsible for Presentation Slide (List slide number/subject)_____

Presenter's Name_____
Title_____
Responsible for Presentation Slide (List slide number/subject)_____

Presenter's Name_____
Title_____
Responsible for Presentation Slide (List slide number/subject)_____

Presenter's Name_____
Title_____
Responsible for Slide/Whiteboard Presentation (List slide number/subject)_____

Goal of Presentation_____
_____

What does the prospect want to see/hear at the meeting?_____

Current product/service being used by the prospect_____
_____

Current business pain with existing product or service_____
_____

What do we want to sell them?_____

What is the dollar value for the first year?_____

What is the dollar value of this client over the next three years?___

Do they have a budget?   _____Yes _____No

If yes, how much?_____

When do they want this product or service?_____

Why will they buy from us?_____

Why will we lose this deal?_____

Which contact is signing the purchase order/contract?_____

Which contact(s) is (are) making the decision?_____

Is there a consultant involved?   _____Yes   _____No
        If yes, what is the consultant's name?_____
        Consultant's company name_____
        Consultant's telephone_____
        Is the consultant: For us_____ Against us_____ Neutral

What are the prospect's business consequences if they do not buy
from us?_____
_____

What does the selling team need to do to close this business?___
_____

Are there any unusual marketing expenses needed to close this
business?_____
_____

Next Action Steps_____

Figure 6.   *Presentation Talking Points form.* As part of
            your Value Forward Tool Box, you should
            complete this form and hand it to each of your
            team members prior to the one-hour executive
            meeting.

Planning for the Three Box Monty™ Executive Presentation

It is essential to plan for any presentation. Below is a format I use that is helpful in organizing the content.

Three Box Monty™	
Executive Presentation Format	
Length: 1 - 1½ hours	
Team Prep	**Minutes**
• Presenter group arrives at least 30 minutes early. Meets in parking lot.	30
Presentation	
1. Presenter introductions/business cards are handed out.	--
2. Introduce attendees.	**5**
3. Lead presenter (salesperson) confirms the amount of time available for the presentation.	
4. Lead presenter reconfirms the business pains expressed by the management contact coupled with industry pains.	**5**
5. Lead presenter launches into slide presentation (eight slides or less) giving company history, client list, and sales value proposition.	**10**
6. Three Box Monty™ presentation (depending on if you have a product or specialized service to explain).	**15-30**
7. Optional step: Service or product presenter launches into physical demo of product or service that is being sold. If not, move on to Step 8.	
8. Executive Briefing Close	**10**
Client Q and A. Wrap-up. Ask transactional questions of the senior executive to confirm he/she is still qualified.	

Figure 7. ***Three Box Monty™ Executive Presentation Format.*** This schedule will help you plan and execute your presentation.

If you follow this format, you can manage all issues that come up, including:

- Presenters arriving late

- The management attendees deciding to stay only thirty minutes and not informing you ahead of time

- Forgetting the names of the attendees who are at the meeting, and not knowing their titles

- Having multiple presenters respond to tough questions differently

- Not leaving enough time for the presentation and Q & A

- Your presentation team not looking or acting as a team

Small Businesses. Even if you are doing a solo presentation, this format will help you maintain a logical progression during the presentation. Studies of sales presentation methods show that when two or more people make a presentation together, statistically they have a higher closing ratio than a solo presenter. So, even if you are a small sales organization, you may want to try a team sale to increase your success.

Using the Three Box Monty™ for Your Executive Briefing

Once you have held a pre-meeting with your sales team, you are ready to go to the prospect's site and hold a Three Box Monty™ presentation. The Three Box Monty™ executive presentation model is about using premeditative selling techniques that make your presentation look like it is spontaneous. It allows the prospect to experience your presentation and ultimately your product and service value. It will also allow you to ask specific questions to determine if the prospect is an active buyer or a passive buyer.

Executive briefing rooms are usually designed in one of the following five formats:

1. **Classroom Setup**—all seating faces forward

2. **Stadium-Style Setup**—seating faces forward, but the seats scale upward from the presenter

3. **Conference-Table Setup**—seating is at a central conference table; usually with a whiteboard or flip chart

4. **Office-Desk Setup**—you present to a manager in his/her office across his/her desk

5. **U-shaped Setup**—seating is in a half-circle around the presenter

**When more than two management team prospects
are in the room, the preferred method for the
Three Box Monty™ is U-shaped seating.** Why?
Because you want to use the room's physical
characteristics and architecture to engage the prospects
during the presentation. This setup entices prospects
into action steps to buy. This is called *room psychology.*
Room psychology is a business tool that most
salespeople forget.

The typical sales presentation is one to three
salespeople in business suits marching into a briefing
room, sitting at a conference table, making an
electronic presentation of their product (or service),
ready to discuss their business value. But this format
makes you look like a commodity and makes it
difficult for the management team to distinguish you
from your competition. Vendors who use this format
end up looking the same.

By using a U-shaped seating environment, you can
move around the presentation room and control the
attention of the prospect as you communicate your
specific business value. When you use the room as a
business tool, you change the dynamics of the room.
Instead of being *just another vendor,* you are now
someone who demands attention and increases their
attentiveness of what you have to say. If you have a
choice or the flexibility of rearranging the presentation

environment, use a U-shaped room for greater success.

Here are some key points to remember when using the Three Box Monty™:

▶ The Three Box Monty™ is designed to last no longer than one and a half hours, with one hour being the optimum amount of time for your presentation.

▶ Your overhead presentation should have no more than eight slides.

▶ Do not hand out company brochures at your presentation because it is distracting to the prospect.

▶ Hand out a one-page document with three blank boxes on it to each attendee before you start your discussion (see Figure 5).

▶ At the end of the Three Box Monty™, your goal is to ask the senior executive for a proposal or purchase order, or alternatively to set up a more detailed discovery meeting based on what kind of product or service you sell and decide whether the prospect is an active buyer or a passive buyer. Remember, in Value Forward Selling, we move prospects back and forth between an active and passive buyer status based on the action steps they take.

▶ The Three Box Monty™ is an interactive executive presentation designed to distinguish your value and to position you differently from your competition.

▶ During the presentation, the salesperson **always stands**! This positions you like a teacher and your prospects like students (just like in school).

▶ If you are presenting with a sales team, team members should ask your pre-determined questions to the prospects during the presentation.

▶ The goal of the Three Box Monty™ is to engage the prospects as business peers and drive them to action steps that move them to the next step of your sales cycle (i.e., a proposal, a business discovery meeting, a pilot, a purchase order, etc.).

Three Box Monty Phase One. (Length: 15 minutes) When you enter the room, pass out your materials, including your business card and the one-page blank form; set up your overhead presentation devices; introduce yourself and your team; and gather the prospects' business cards.

As mentioned previously, you as the salesperson on this account should *never* sit down, but your team should sit down. This is crucial for room psychology. As you stand above your management audience, they become subordinate to you physically and ultimately psychologically. This gives you power over all of the attendees.

Most people in management positions have gone to college or a university and learned how to take notes in a seated subordinate position. So, as soon as you stand before them, subliminally they regress and become students, better listeners, and more informed buyers. You are now on stage selling your value.

By becoming students again, they open up their minds and allow themselves to listen to what you have to say. Additionally, by the very fact of not sitting down, you immediately look different from all of the other vendors and the prospect's retention of your material will be greater.

Salespeople often wonder if they should ask management attendees what they would like to see during the presentation. The answer is, of course, yes they should ask what the prospect would like to see. However, you should collect this information *before* you give the Three Box Monty™ presentation. If you ask management at the start of the presentation, you could waste twenty to thirty minutes of your valuable one-hour time allotment and the senior executive in the room may leave early. So, control the time you have by confirming what you have been told is expected and ask if there are any additional requests. Knowing what the prospect wants to hear is important. But try to get this information before the briefing.

After everyone has been introduced and you have passed out your paperwork and business cards, give your overhead slide presentation (or just speak) to the management team about your company. If you use electronic overhead presentation technology, remember that your presentation should be **no more than eight slides**—no matter what your marketing or operations department says. Showing a twenty-five-slide deck will put your management prospects to sleep.

Management does not like to sit through electronic presentations. Walking into an executive presentation and showing a twenty- to forty-slide show will turn them off and make you look like another vendor. Your opening presentation should include the following:

- Your company history

- Your sales value proposition

- Your current client list

- An overview of your product or service programs

NOTE: The best time to do executive presentations is between 9:30 a.m. and 11:00 a.m. your prospect's time. This is after breakfast and before lunch and most people are at a high energy level. Giving a briefing after lunch exposes you to lower attention spans and less success.

During this presentation, **the rest of your team is seated**. Once you have completed the first section, the standing lead salesperson walks to the front of the presentation room and says,

> *So far we have talked about our firm, our history, and why we are specialists. Now let's look at what's going on in your industry (name their industry).*

At this point, walk over to a whiteboard or an easel and draw three squares, using the same format as they appear on the piece of paper you handed out . Once you draw the three boxes on the whiteboard, your entire audience will now look at the blank piece of paper and recognize that it matches the whiteboard (see Figure 8).

Three Box Monty Phase Two. (Length: 30 minutes) In the top left box write the industry you are presenting to. For example, if you are trying to sell to manufacturing wholesalers, write the words "Manufacturing Wholesalers." If you are selling software to the healthcare industry, write "Healthcare."

After you have written your prospect's industry in Box 1, walk away from the whiteboard toward your audience and say:

> *Because we are specialists in [INSERT YOUR SALES VALUE PROPOSITION] we monitor the [INSERT YOUR PROSPECT'S INDUSTRY] industry's ongoing business events (never say the word problems because some prospects think they never have problems). Currently ABC research [INSERT A THIRD-PARTY RESEARCH INDUSTRY COMPANY NAME, INDUSTRY TRADE MAGAZINES, ETC.] has observed that there are five main business events affecting the [INSERT THEIR INDUSTRY]. They include . . .*

Then return to the whiteboard and list five to seven business issues in a bullet format currently affecting their industry under Box 1. Make sure the industry issues are business pains your product or service can fix.

Example for Healthcare Industry

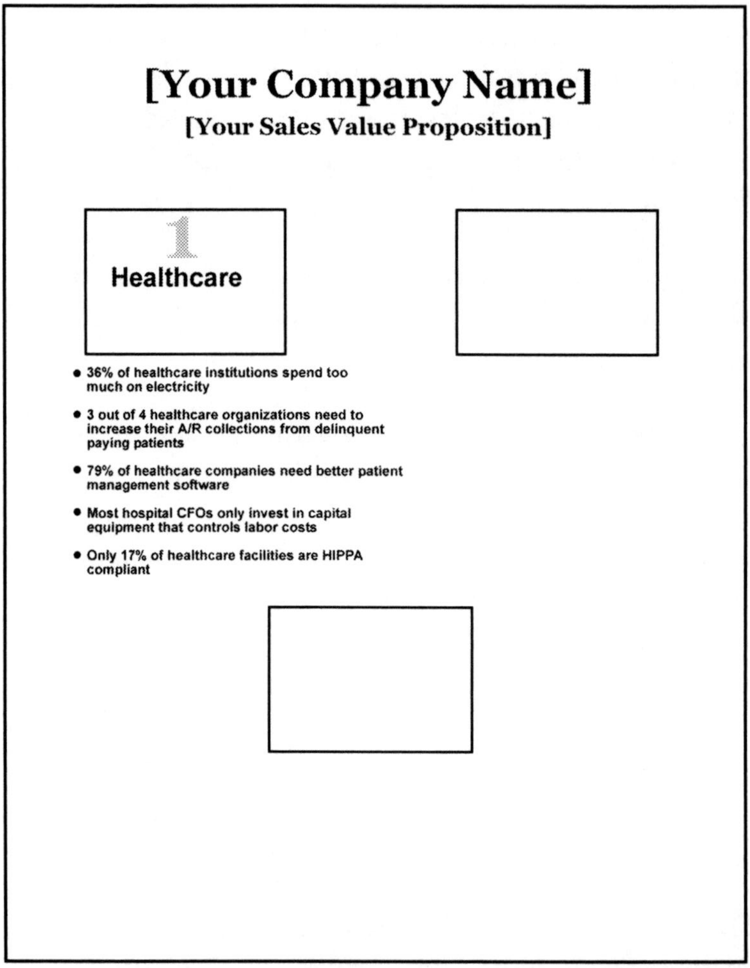

[Your Company Name]

[Your Sales Value Proposition]

1

Healthcare

- 36% of healthcare institutions spend too much on electricity

- 3 out of 4 healthcare organizations need to increase their A/R collections from delinquent paying patients

- 79% of healthcare companies need better patient management software

- Most hospital CFOs only invest in capital equipment that controls labor costs

- Only 17% of healthcare facilities are HIPPA compliant

Figure 8. *Three Box Monty™—Box 1.* As you launch into your presentation, the industry box is the first box you will expand on.

After you have listed these bullets on the whiteboard, **walk away from the whiteboard toward the audience and say:**

> *Based on what you see here on the board, are there any other [INSERT THEIR INDUSTRY] events currently affecting your industry?*

Wait for their answer. When the first person voices an example not on your list, walk over and hand him/her the marker and say, *That's great. Can you put that on the board under the industry box, please?*

Fifty percent of the time, no matter what the title of the person is, they will get up and place their response on the whiteboard under the industry box. Why? It is crowd control. It is psychological pressure to respond and conform.

What are you doing?

Instead of having a traditional buy my product or service presentation, you are creating an *experiential sales presentation* so the prospect will experience your value as a participant, not as an observer. If the prospect does not stand up, don't worry about it, just walk over to the whiteboard and write his/her suggestion under the industry box (Box 1).

An amazing thing is happening during your executive Three Box Monty™ presentation. Remember the blank piece of paper you handed out at the beginning of the meeting? Your prospects are now writing what you put on the whiteboard onto their blank pieces of paper, word for word! You are controlling the notes your prospects are taking about your product or service.

What do prospects read first after they have seen a vendor's presentation? Not the vendor's brochures. Not the vendor's pre-written handout. *Their own notes in their handwriting.*

Whatever you write on the whiteboard under the three boxes, your prospects will copy on their paper under the boxes because they observe everyone doing it and because they want to know what's going on.

After the prospect's suggestion is written on the whiteboard (or if no one gives you a suggestion), move onto Box 2. In the middle of the top right box write the prospect's company name.

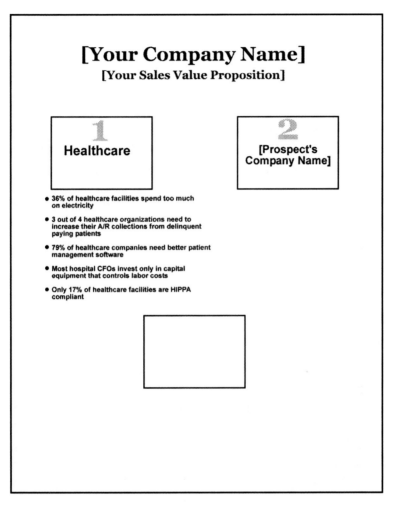

Figure 9. *Three Box Monty™—Box 2.* As you build your presentation, the prospect's box is the second box you will expand on.

After you have written the company name in the middle of Box 2, walk away from the whiteboard and say to your audience:

Based on my conversation with John Smith [NAME THE EXECUTIVE YOU MET WITH DURING YOUR TWENTY-MINUTE MEETING], your firm is currently looking to adjust the following areas . . .

Now name two or three business pains you discussed during your original twenty-minute meeting under Box 2.

NOTE: It is essential *not* to say, *I know what your firm needs to adjust (or fix),* because if you do, someone from the prospect's company is going to question how you know. Reinforce that you were *told* about the prospect's business pains from the manager you met with previously.

Next, write down the business issues communicated to you by the executive under Box 2.

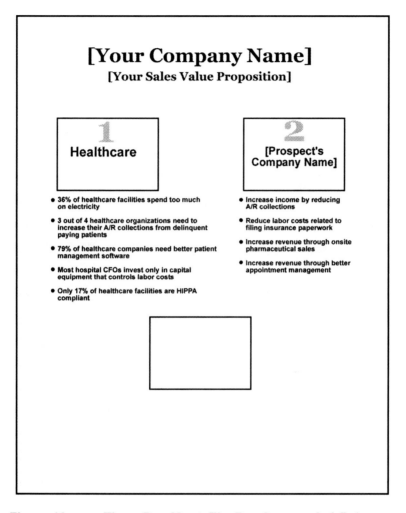

Figure 10. *Three Box Monty™—Box 2 expanded.* Below the company name, write a list of business issues your prospect has communicated to you.

When you have written two or more business events affecting the company under Box 2, again walk away from the whiteboard and ask your prospects (while still standing), *Are there any other business areas you feel your firm needs to work on?*

If anyone answers, walk over, hand him the marker, and ask him to write his suggestion on the whiteboard under Box 2. Again, observe how everyone in the room writes on their blank piece of paper.

Once you have listed the information under Box 2, proceed to Box 3 (your company box) and list how your products or services will fix the prospect's business issues or events listed underneath Box 2.

[Your Company Name]
[Your Sales Value Proposition]

1

Healthcare

- 36% of healthcare facilities spend too much on electricity

- 3 out of 4 healthcare organizations need to increase their A/R collections from delinquent paying patients

- 79% of healthcare companies need better patient management software

- Most hospital CFOs invest only in capital equipment that controls labor costs

- Only 17% of healthcare facilities are HIPPA compliant

2

[Prospect's Company Name]

- Increase income by reducing A/R collections

- Reduce labor costs related to filing insurance paperwork

- Increase revenue through onsite pharmaceutical sales

- Increase revenue through better appointment management

3

[Your Company]

- Engage client in best practices strategy consulting

- Install new software application to automate insurance claims

- Install automated telephone collection system for patient collection

- Train physicians on revenue management

Figure 11. ***Three Box Monty™—Box 3.*** The final part of building your presentation is under Box 3, where you list how your company will help the prospect reach their goals.

As you complete your presentation, connect each of the boxes with arrows. This will pull together the industry events, prospect events, and your firm's

ability to fix the prospect's pain. Your finished
presentation should look similar to this:

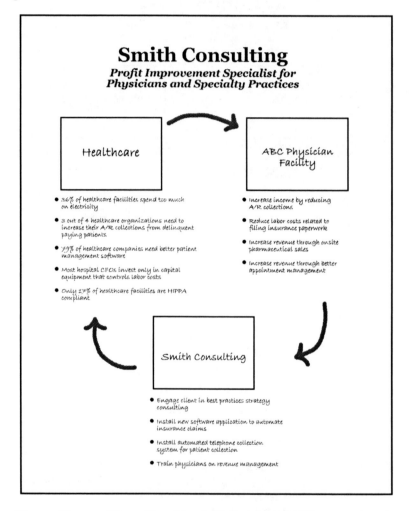

Figure 12. ***Three Box Monty™ Completed.*** The completed
Three Box Monty™ does not include the
numbered references we use in this book to
explain the process.

During the Three Box Monty™ presentation, **make sure your sales team asks the prepared questions of the respective prospect attendees**. Although it was premeditated in its preparation, the *spontaneous* questions during the presentation help engage the prospect. Remember, you are still standing. As you lead the presentation by walking around the room, the prospect's eyes and thoughts follow you, increasing their absorption of your offering's value.

After you have listed how you will help the prospects fix their business issues under Box 3, walk away from the whiteboard and ask, *Is there anything else my firm can do to help you fix these events listed under Box 2?*

If any suggestions are given, list them on the whiteboard under your observations in Box 3. Once you have finished the Three Box Monty™, you have two options:

- Do a product demo or service discussion in more detail if you sell a product; or

- Move forward to the closing stage.

Case Study—Presenting to Prospects: The Three Box Monty™

I have used the Three Box Monty™ to sell both products and services to Fortune 500 companies. At one such event, when I entered the room to make my executive presentation, there were more than twenty people in the room, including senior vice presidents, a chief financial officer, and multitudes of supervisors.

After I had gone through my eight-slide presentation, I drew the three boxes on a whiteboard and proceeded to talk about the industry in Box 1.

As soon as I named five current business pains in the industry, I walked away from the whiteboard and asked, *Are there any other business events going on in your industry that I have missed?*

A manager with the title of director raised his hand and gave me one more example. I walked over to him and handed him the marker. He wrote his comments down under Box 1.

As soon as he completed this, a vice president got up and took the marker from him and wrote five more business issues under Box 1.

When he sat down, I went to Box 2 and listed all the events currently affecting the prospect that were described to me by the vice president during our previous twenty-minute meeting.

As soon as I finished, the vice president got up in front of his team and added three more events (problems) to Box 2 that were important to them. Before I got to Box 3, the executive I had originally met with started talking about how our products and services would help them fix their company's business issues. Before I could draw a connection between the boxes, the executive (still standing in the front of the room) connected Boxes 2 and 3 (with my firm's company name in it) and for the next fifteen minutes told his management team how "we" were going to help them improve their business operations.

With the vice president leading my presentation, all I could hear was "Ka Ching, Ka Ching" in the back of my mind, because at that point I knew they were going to buy from me.

Why?

> Because I focused on their business pains and needs. I had become a **pain management specialist** and I had used the Three Box Monty™ experiential sales presentation so the management team could experience the value of our products and services.
>
> Use the Three Box Monty™ with any size company and management team. It works with small privately-held companies and billion-dollar conglomerates.

Wrapping Up the Three Box Monty™ Presentation

Once you move forward to the executive briefing closing stage, you are going into a *transactional sales methodology.* Your Three Box Monty™ executive briefing is a *value forward* approach that demonstrates your business value based on your knowledge of the industry's business pain, the prospect company's business pain, and how your company will fix these pains.

As you move into the executive briefing closing stage (still standing), you are going to take the senior contact through a questioning process that requires you to be blunt.

Your position as a peer instead of a vendor opens the door for you to ask specific direct questions. This process of being *professionally blunt* is an earned process. You can't ask these questions of management until you have earned the right and you have earned the right if you've made it this far. And, once you have earned the right, it is your job to prove that the prospect is a *qualified buyer*. You do not want to continue in this sales cycle with a professional looker, so it is imperative that your professionally blunt questions drive accurate answers. With accurate answers, you can then decide if you should move forward with the prospect or put them into a passive buying mode. (Remember, you are still standing during the presentation.)

When using the Three Box Monty™, wrap up your presentation by following these steps:

1. After you have finished, walk away from the whiteboard toward the senior executive in the room.

2. Walk to the senior executive and stand four to six feet away from him. If the room is circular, walk down the aisle along the wall to be physically near the executive. If people are sitting at a conference table, walk down the aisle to be near the senior executive. **This is critical.**

3. When you are within range, look at the senior executive and ask the following questions:

   Mr. Prospect, based on what you have seen and heard today, would you like to receive a proposal [have a specification discovery meeting, demo, to buy, etc.] from us?

By asking the senior executive this question while you are standing above him within four to six feet, you are psychologically putting pressure on him to answer publicly, in front of his peers and subordinates, with an honest and straightforward answer.

If you were to ask this from a sitting position at the other end of the conference room, you would lose your positional strength. Standing and asking this question is not too aggressive or intimidating if you have been walking around during the entire presentation. Be sure to ask the questions politely and in a controlled low tone of voice.

By using the power of the room, physical distance, and blunt questions in a public arena, you will drive the senior executive to tell you the truth.

At this point, one of two things will happen:

- They love your sales value proposition and want a proposal (or a more detailed product or service demonstration); or

- They will get back to you.

Either way, before you leave, ask the senior executive in the room, "*What is the next step?*"

If he says he would like to receive a proposal, **do not** ask who to send it to. Always hand-deliver proposals to the senior executive or the president of the small firm. The reason for this is that you want to continue the sales process with the decision maker you started with. You do not want to be relegated to a lower level.

When you finish the proposal, you will call the executive and deliver it in person, giving you the opportunity to present and discuss it.

If he says, *Thank you for your time. We will get back to you,* **while you're still standing**, ask the senior executive in the room, *Do you think there is a good fit for our two firms to work together?* Listen carefully. He may be seeking input from others and just wants to regroup at a private meeting to get their input. Or, the executive may not be interested and is waiting to tell you in an easier format (on the phone).

Remember, *fifty percent of all sales are won or lost in the executive presentation.* If you're selling jewelry, wholesale supplies, pharmaceuticals, electronics, software, or services, this is the most important step of your sales cycle. This is not a time to be passive. If you leave the room without a good, strong feeling about how it went, you lose. If you get a weak response, you probably did not present well. Ask the senior executive two more questions:

1. *Mr. Executive, is there any additional information that my team could supply you to help you consider our firm?*

2. *Mr. Executive, would you like to get a proposal from us?*

Ask these questions to prod for more feedback on where you stand. Nobody wants to spend time and effort on a proposal for a client that is not interested. The executive's response is what you are seeking. You need to understand his hesitation in order to address his objections.

You are now in a world with decision makers and decision influencers. Ask TOUGH QUESTIONS politely, and ask for their business *now!*

The executive may respond in one of four following ways:

1. *Yes, Paul, we are interested in moving forward and would like to get a proposal.* If you hear this answer (still standing), ask these qualifying questions again:

   o *Is your budget still between $30,000 and $70,000, as we originally discussed?*

  o *Are you still looking to have inventory in your warehouse (software, bicycles, pharmaceuticals) by June?*

2. *At this time Paul, we would like to regroup and decide amongst ourselves and get back to you.* Again, ask the above qualifying questions (previously discussed during the 20-minute meeting), but framed with their response:

  o *Based on our earlier conversations, is your budget still between $30,000 and $70,000?*

  o *Are you still looking to have inventory in your warehouse (software, bicycles, pharmaceuticals) by June?*

  o *When will you make your decision on the vendor short list?*

By focusing on the qualifying questions, even when the prospects will not commit, you continually push them to validate that they are buyers, not professional lookers (over and over). This is the key to selling more.

3. *Paul, at this time we require more service detail information (a detailed demo, discovery meeting, scoping meeting, product pilot, service description).* You may hear this depending on the complexities of what you sell. When the prospect says this to you,

move forward with your qualifying questions, again framed by their response:

o *Mr. Prospect, if we successfully demonstrate our product (or service) strengths in a follow-up meeting for you, with your department heads, do you want us to submit a proposal with detailed pricing?*

o *Do you still have a budget between $30,000 and $70,000?*

o *Are you still looking to have inventory in your warehouse (software, bicycles, pharmaceuticals) by June?*

Again, focus on qualifying the prospect to validate that they are buyers.

4. *At this time Paul, we are not interested in moving forward with your company.* Many salespeople fear this kind of response. But, in fact, it is better for the executive to say this now, rather than later and lose the deal because of the prospect's team talking privately about you at the water cooler. Public disclosure of not wanting to move forward by the prospect is a strategic tool to help you manage your sales cycle.

Maybe they did not understand what you sell or maybe you failed to express how your product or service would increase income, decrease expenses, or manage risks well enough for them to see the value of your offer. When a manager responds with this, just say:

Mr. Prospect, I am surprised. Why don't you want to move forward with our product (or service) proposal?

Based on the effort you have put in so far, you have earned the right to be professionally blunt and deserve an honest answer. You must get the executive to tell you why they do not want to move forward so you can respond.

Regardless of the reasoning, you must now deal with sales objections. Remember, you are the sales professional. If you try to manage sales objections later through one of the management team's subordinates, you will not be effective. They are not professional salespeople and whatever you say to them will be filtered and adjusted based on their education, communication skills, and vendor bias.

Many deals are lost when a salesperson communicates a response to a sales objection through a non-sales contact. *They are not you.*

Use the Three Box Monty™ to drive management prospects to prove they are qualified buyers and that you are not wasting your valuable selling time chasing rainbows with prospects who are lookers, not buyers. You have earned the right.

Follow-Up. After the meeting, send *everyone* a thank-you note, reconfirming the following:

- Your sales value proposition

- The industry pains

- Their pains as illustrated on the whiteboard

- Your firm's ability to fix those pains

Make the letter no longer than two pages and send it in a priority mail envelope (not folded). It will get noticed because of the hard container yet it is less expensive than overnight delivery.

Tips for Whiteboard Presentations

1. By standing up at the whiteboard while your prospects sit down and listen, you have taken a superior-subordinate position over them. By standing above them, you are the teacher and they are the students. That's why the aggressive prospect in the presentation room will quiet down when you hand him the whiteboard marker to put his thoughts on the whiteboard. Now, instead of feeling insecure and

subordinate, he gets to stand up and feel equal again.

2. When speaking in a standing position, always repeat an important message. Say the message a second time, lean forward with emphasis, and speak half as fast as you did the first time.

We are specialists in milestone management!
We are specialists in milestone management!

3. Take public speaking courses to reinforce your sales training skills. Remember, if you are selling to a roomful of executives, they will all take notes and then go back to their offices. You need to *paint a visual brochure* in their minds (and in their notes) of your company's unique sales value proposition. When they regroup as a decision team or a steering committee, they will remember you and your firm favorably.

Case Study—Presenting to Prospects: Small Business Presentation Variation

I was meeting with the president and CFO of a fifty-person company in their conference room to sell them a product. As soon as I finished my company overview and our sales value proposition, I went to his whiteboard and drew the three boxes.

I then handed the president the marker and asked him what events (business pains) he saw in his industry facing the small business owner. He then went to the whiteboard and under the industry box he started listing the industry issues.

We chatted about what he wrote. When he was finished, I handed the marker to the CFO and asked him to list some of the issues and events he was experiencing. The CFO then listed them under his box (remember income-expense-risk control).

> With that completed, I went to my firm's box and listed underneath how we could fix these pains. Then I connected the three boxes with arrows. By having the management executives in this small firm visualize with me their problems and my firm's ability to be a doctor to fix their problems, I had simultaneously eliminated all of my competition and won the deal.

The Three Box Monty™ is a professional communication tool that uses a value forward technique to position you and your firm as specialists. It creates an impression in the buyer's mind that you are a peer and someone they should work with.

Case Study—Presenting to Prospects: Fortune 1000 Presentation

A team consisting of three support and operations staff members and myself were presenting at one of the largest discount department store chains in the world at their corporate headquarters.

There were about twenty people in the room, including the CFO, the CIO, and the CTO. The CTO was well recognized in business magazines as a world leader and visionary and was the dominant personality in the room.

I went through the steps listed above. During our meeting, the CTO was aggressive in his questioning about my sales value proposition and what made us different. At the opening of the presentation, I did a five-slide computer overhead presentation about our background, our customers, and my central sales value proposition. As each slide was presented, the CTO asked detailed, long-winded questions, probing and pushing for details.

At the end of the slide presentation, I went to the whiteboard, drew the three boxes, listed the industry's pains, and then I turned to the executive and said, *Mr. CTO, what additional pain is your industry experiencing?*

The CTO got up and started a ten-minute dissertation of the industry's issues. As he spoke, he listed these issues under the industry box. When he was finished (and still standing at the whiteboard), I then said *Mr. CTO, what industry issues is your firm experiencing?*

The CTO proceeded to list his firm's issues under his company's box. Simultaneously, the CTO started asking for input from his management team sitting in the audience. As I stood there, next to the CTO, in the front of the room of this multi-billion dollar company, he started convincing himself and his team how our two companies could work together. When the CTO was finished, I listed and discussed our pain management features under our box and then connected them with arrows.

As soon as I had connected the boxes, the CTO got up again from his seat, went to the whiteboard and laid out a complete rollout of my products and their operations to his management team. Guess who got the deal?

The whiteboard method works. Try it. You will win more deals!

Using Slide Presentations

Generally, slide presentations are not used during the initial twenty-minute meeting for several reasons:

- Slides are distracting to the decision maker

- Using slides makes it difficult to maintain your self-imposed twenty-minute allotment

- Valuable time is wasted setting up and taking down your PC

- The meeting will seem more like a sales call than a discussion among equals

Remember, the twenty-minute meeting is a *conceptual* sale. The term *professional slide presentation* is an oxymoron. Even though professional salespeople use them quite often, their usage increasingly annoys executives. Professional speakers are reverting back to a whiteboard to communicate information because this method is more interactive.

My rule of thumb is not to use a slide presentation unless you have to. When you do, keep it short. The higher the title of the manager you are presenting to, the fewer slides you should show. If you use a slide presentation at your second meeting, use these guidelines:

- Slide presentations are talking points, not reading points.

- For CEO presentations, use five slides or less.

- For VP presentations, use eight slides or less.

- Each slide should contain a two-minute Talking Point.

- No slide should have more than three arrows on it.

- All fonts should be at least 24 point in size.

- Use more graphics (not graphs) and fewer words.

- Use no more than six words per line; no more than six lines per slide. This is called the **Rule of 6**.

Using Portfolio Presentations

Small Businesses. If you are selling a product or service to small businesses, you may be asked during your first meeting to present your portfolio. You should always carry images or screen shots of your product or service in a large art folder, but do not take them out unless asked to. The key is to keep the conversation strategic rather than tactical.

If the client pushes to see your work, it is better to show screen shots or images because it is important to *control the client in every sales meeting*, rather than allowing the client to control you. If you verbally inform the client of specific products or services your firm has worked on, they will focus on what you offer, not how your product or service can help their business.

If the client pushes you to show product or service features early in the conversation, continue your dialogue about your sales value proposition and on how your product or service goals are designed to increase income, decrease expenses, or manage risks.

By following this process, you can turn their tactical questions (to see your work) into a strategic opening to reinforce your sales value proposition.

As you discuss your sales value proposition, open up your presentation folder and point to a specific picture or example of your product or service. Again, focus on how your product or service (directly or indirectly) can *strategically* increase revenue, decrease expenses, or manage risks.

Always talk about your product or service value **before** you show it. Repeat this method several times until the executive gets it. This presentation process is so different from what your average small business salesperson does that it will win you respect and the attention of the president. And it is crucial to creating a perception of value. The more you focus on your product or service's offerings, the more the prospect will see you and what you offer as a commodity. It is not *how* the product or service is used but *why* the product or services should be used!

Keep in mind many management teams do not know how to buy correctly. As a salesperson you need to adjust your skills to make up for the buyer's inability to understand your value over your competition's value.

Chapter 7
Presenting to Prospects – The Executive Briefing

Review and Exercises

1. Type out talking points for your next meeting or presentation.

2. When you find yourself planning a meeting with several team members, prepare a script so everyone can participate in the topic that they are most knowledgeable about.

3. Review the mining questions you developed in Chapter 6 before your next meeting

4. Experiment with a whiteboard and learn to feel comfortable drawing and working with it.

5. Review any slide presentations before you use them. Copy the presentation and rename it to reflect a shorter version. VP presentations should have no more than ten slides; CEO presentations should have no more than five slides. If your presentation is longer than these parameters, shorten it to the respective number of slides. Apply the *Rule of 6* and develop the presentation as a supporting mechanism to your conversation, not a distraction. You don't want the executive to be distracted by the volume of information and trying to read the mass of information that is found in vendor presentations. You're a peer now—it is time to start presenting like one.

Chapter 7
Presenting to Prospects – The Executive Briefing

Chapter 8

Preparing a Management Proposal That Works

After reading this chapter, you will know:

- How to submit a professional proposal to management

- How to use psychological ROI to close deals

- Why price is not always relevant

- How to handle requests for proposals (RFPs)

Management Proposal Basics

Like business plans submitted to banks, venture capitalists, and business buyers, you must submit proposals with detail that is consumable, specific or to the point, and focused on the prospect's needs. Most vendor proposals are too long, too technical, and do not focus on the buyer's needs. Selling to management is not about the vendor. **It is about the buyer.**

Remember, your proposal is the invisible *salesperson* who is allowed into the boardroom when management talks about your offering. If done correctly, this invisible salesperson will consistently communicate a structured value to the decision makers. Your proposal should convey your *value forward* message succinctly so that anyone picking up your proposal would understand the prospects' business problems and the ability for your product or service to fix it.

Word density is a prevalent communication method used by many salespeople today. Salespeople spurned on by their operations, technical, marketing, and strategy departments often get immersed in company vernacular that is unique to their firm. When they meet management buyers, they drop these company abbreviations, product or service description nomenclatures, and *industry speak* during their sales presentations, which often turns off buyers. This over usage of vendor terminology should be avoided, especially in business proposals. When selling management, minimize your word density.

Buyers don't care about you. They care about themselves. Using company-developed language gets in the way of your sales cycle. If your product or service is the called the *ABS Care Program*, the *FAMed Software Module*, the *ManNam Service Program* or some other made up name, and your prospect cannot readily identify how it will fix her business needs, then you are wasting your sales time.

Take the following word density test and evaluate your current sales letters, brochures, proposals, and overhead presentations to see if your corporate communications are helping you sell or creating barriers for management buyers to understand what and why they should work with you.

Word Density Analysis

To determine and reduce the word density in your sales, marketing, presentation, proposals, and closing documents, you should:

1. Collect all of the e-mails you have sent to targeted prospects during the last ninety days.

2. Collect all of the sales letters you have sent to your prospects during the last ninety days.

3. Collect all of your company brochures and proposals.

4. Get a copy of your company's electronic media presentations.

5. Circle the words that describe the programs or services specifically used by your firm. How many technical and company words have slipped into your sales communication with your prospects?

6. Reduce your word density by cutting back on operations' technical verbiage and focusing on pain management.

It's your sale.

It's your commission.

You need to review **every** proposal (especially if you are in a big company). Many firms use a generic proposal. Generic proposals do not win business—an important point when packaging a management proposal.

Always restate in the proposal the information that you gave in your personal presentation, using the following format:

- Identify client pains and place them in the body of the proposal or as a footnote that reminds the prospect, *as supplied at our meeting . . .*

- List your sales value proposition

- Describe your firm's history

- List key contacts in your company

- List your clients

- List industry pain issues

- Make sure the proposal is readable for anyone who is non-technical (assume the CFO will be reading it) and put all of the technical specifications in the back under a separate heading

- List the description of products or services

- State the implementation or rollout schedule

- Provide a list of deployment/practice team/support members by name assigned to the prospect's account

- Describe how your product or service will help the management team increase income, decrease expenses, or manage risks

- List client benefits (psychological return on investment—discussed on the next page)

- Provide explanations to justify pricing on the pricing page

- Provide a conclusion of why they should buy

Small to Medium Businesses. If you are selling to companies with less than one hundred employees, always overproduce your proposal presentation to the senior executive. It is not who you are; *it is who they perceive you to be.*

Executive Proposal Pitch

The entire Value Forward Selling program is based on the premeditated process of thinking through each step of the sales process and then packaging the actions required to close the sale.

Many salespeople try to show their productivity to managers by generating a bunch of proposals and sending them to prospective clients. These proposals are added to the manager's corporate sales forecasts and tend to sit in the prospect's inbox while the manager and the salesperson impatiently wait for the sale to be approved. Wrong!

When possible, do not send management proposals by e-mail. E-mail has ruined the closing ratio of prospects. Professional sales executives should never e-mail a proposal to a senior executive if the dollar value of the proposal warrants it. All proposals should be delivered personally and explained in a follow-up meeting. **Again, manage the client; don't allow the client to manage you**.

When your proposal is completed, phone the executive and say:

> *Mr./Ms. X, per your request, our proposal is ready. I would like to meet with you for thirty minutes to go through the details. It will be quick, but there are some unique areas in this*

*proposal that we have included based on your
input and your needs (list his firm's pains)
discussed in our presentation. I normally meet
with executives such as yourself [or insert their
title] for thirty minutes to discuss proposals in
person.*

Invite them to lunch. **Get a meeting to hand deliver
the proposal and then discuss with them the value
you bring.**

Psychological ROI

The strongest method for closing sales is *psychological
return on investment (psychological ROI).* Stronger than
financial ROI, it plays to the decision maker's personal
needs and pains. Using psychological ROI instead of
financial ROI propels you past the average product or
service salesperson into the heavy-hitter category.

I have used this process with management executives
of Fortune 1000 companies and with presidents of
ten-person firms. It doesn't matter how big or small a
company is, it works. It will help you close
management deals and increase your income.

Psychological ROI is rooted in the same premise
echoed throughout this book. You *must* be dealing
with the decision maker or management for this
process to work. Management executives, like you,

have personal expectations, fears, and goals that drive business decisions on a daily basis. Many times, they make these decisions independent of business logic of features, price, or service functions.

Remember, management makes decisions based on their impressions of your value and consequence communication can be an effective tool for you to drive vendor selection to your camp. Management buys on emotion.

The concept of financial ROI was invented by vendors who could not cost-justify their proposals to prospects. In fact, sales organizations have used this as a sales tool so often during the last twenty years that prospects are now trained to ask for it as a purchase criterion.

Yet, more and more executives are discounting financial ROI because of the inability to use it as a tool to objectively qualify vendors. Many business magazines have discussed how vendor supplied ROI is becoming less and less important.

So, what tools can a salesperson use to sell more?

Psychological ROI is a process of communicating business value based on the **senior executive's personal needs as well as his business needs**—not just the firm's needs.

It is a subtle approach involving the prospect's fears and anxieties of buying correctly and the consequences of what happens if he makes an incorrect vendor selection or no selection at all. This is not a new technique, but one that has been used for many years.

Have you ever lost a deal to a competitor that did not make any logical sense? The competitor's price was higher, their product was inferior, their firm was smaller, and/or they had bad references. This is a result of the prospect buying because of psychological ROI factors.

This happens every day in general sales. People buy life insurance, drive safe cars, use body fragrance, and eat healthy foods based on the psychological fear of the consequences from making the wrong decision or no decision at all.

This method can be used to sell to Fortune 1000 management and to CEOs of small private firms. After all, executives are human. They have phobias, insecurities, house mortgages, bosses, investors, and a need to belong and be accepted. When selling to management, use psychological ROI to increase your closing ratio. **Psychological ROI levels the playing field for all vendors.** It is not biased toward large companies, small firms, established vendors, or new players. The success of psychological ROI is totally dependent upon the salesperson's ability to understand the intersection of the prospect's business needs with the prospect's personal needs.

Once this intersection is discovered, you can use specific parallel image communication with the prospect to increase your sales success by positioning your offering as a preferred choice with the best purchase consequences for the firm **AND** the decision maker.

Often, salespeople focus only on the prospect's business needs and forget about the prospect's personal needs, thereby reducing the ability to close more deals. Psychological ROI elements are not normally communicated to you directly, like conditions of sale listed in a Request for Proposal (RFP).

But prospect fears exist, and they can be discovered and used as a business-selling tool. By understanding and managing the personal needs of any prospect simultaneously with the business needs of the prospect's employer, you will effectively increase your closing ratio by a factor of two.

Figure 13 on the next page lists some of the psychological sales variables that need to be managed by you during a sales cycle to close more business.

Figure 13. ***Psychological Sales Variables.*** This figure identifies factors that need to be considered when using psychological ROI as a sales tool.

Management does not make business decisions in a vacuum. Like you, they make decisions based on the psychological cues (both direct and indirect) they receive from vendors.

Remember, this is a subtle technique to be used with management. Psychological ROI is not aggressive communication, it's intelligent communication. When dealing with management, there are direct and indirect fears (or consequences) at work (irrational at times) that affect their business judgments, which include:

- Being fired

- Not receiving a raise

- Not receiving a financial bonus

- Not being promoted

- The proposal costs will go over budget

- The proposal will affect other departments' efficiencies

- The vendor recommendation will not fix the pain

- Being embarrassed in front of their subordinates

- Being embarrassed in front of their peers

- Being embarrassed in front of their bosses

- Not getting additional funding from their investors or banks

- Working too much, which affects their personal lives

Additionally, their goals are the reverse of the above list and include:

- Being promoted

- Being praised and noticed (ego driven)

- Increasing revenue

- Spending more time with their families

- Looking better than their peers in a board meeting

Identifying these fears and goals in your communication will give you power. With power, you can position your firm's product or service proposal more positively to differentiate yourself from your competitors. You can identify fears and goals of senior executives through:

- Direct Statements

- Visual Observations

- Judgmental Observations

Direct Statements. Believe it or not, many times a senior executive will actually tell you his issues. You only have to listen.

Here are examples of business consequences prospects are concerned about and have actually shared with me:

▶ My company is depending on this new jewelry wholesale line to help increase our per-store revenue and our stock price. **Vice President, Store Operations**

▶ This strategy consulting service has to work or I'm going to be accountable to the board. **CEO**

▶ The CEO has told me that my entire department budget is at stake if we cannot reduce our overhead. **Vice President, Operations**

▶ I've had this position for six months. The last CIO was let go because he was old school and not progressive. **CIO**

So, listen. Ask questions. Learn what fears they have, and collect information to use in your sales cycle management.

Visual Observations. When you meet in managers' offices for your twenty-minute meeting, look around their offices. Notice the pictures on their desks and the plaques on the walls. Who are they? Who do they want you to think they are? What is important to them?

- Do they have a paperweight shaped like a barbell?

- Do they have a Harvard MBA diploma on the wall?

- Do they have pictures of themselves involved in sports activities, like skiing or skydiving?

- Do they have industry awards or plaques on the wall from trade associations?

All of these visuals provide information to help you determine what motivates this person—both professionally and personally.

Judgmental Observations. Reading the client will help you close the client. Salespeople of all types use these observation tools to sell.

- Are they in good physical shape?

- Do they have leadership appeal?

- Are they intelligent?

Yes, these are all judgment calls that you are going to have to make. *It's your commission at stake.* I am not saying all people can be generalized, but as a salesperson, you must make judgments about people to sell more. Here are some examples:

- Insurance is sold based on the **fear** of not being able to take care of loved ones

- Stock investments are sold based on **the desire to improve one's financial status**

- Expensive cars are sold based on **ego** and social status needs

Based on my personal experiences selling to management, here are some observations to use for **psychological ROI**. If a senior executive displays these items or characteristics:

- Pictures of him/her skydiving, performing martial arts, scuba diving, rock climbing, mountain biking, car racing, or other activity that is adventurous

- Wear expensive custom-made clothing

- Are involved in bodybuilding

- Talk fast

then they are likely to be driven by:

- Ego

- Adventure

- Risk taking

- Quick decisions

You should discuss how your sales value proposition is the right choice based on those variables. You need to appeal to their ego, their need for adventure, and their desire for risk taking. For example:

1. *Mr./Ms. Executive, one reason CFOs like you invest in our service is because they want us to provide them with the best [YOUR SALES VALUE PROPOSITION] to increase their corporate profits.*

2. *Mr./Ms. Executive, one reason firms like yours invest in our product is because we give management executives like yourself personalized service to help maximize corporate profits through our [SALES VALUE PROPOSITION].*

3. *Mr./Ms. Executive, one reason companies like yours invest in our program is because they realize that the Internet will not stand still for anyone. To be successful in this economy, you must think fast and implement quickly or your competitors will eat your customers.*

If executives display some or all of these characteristics:

- Only family pictures

- Smokes a pipe

- Has held the same management position for ten or more years

then they are likely to be driven by:

- Safety concerns

- Security issues

- Patience

- Comfort

Based on these observations, you should discuss how your sales value proposition is the right choice based on those variables. You need to appeal to their need to be secure and comfortable with their decision.

For example:

1. *Mr./Ms. Executive, because our firm is a local player, we specialize in long-term permanent relationships with our clients.*

2. *Mr./Ms. Executive, we assign a dedicated practice manager to your team so you will always have continuity*

of leadership from our firm and you will always know whom to call if you have any questions.

Now before you write or e-mail me that these are vague generalizations about senior executives and their characterizations—*I agree.* But the point is to evaluate the decision maker and use the evaluation process to appeal to their needs in order to close business.

Price Is Not Always Relevant

When selling products and services to senior executives, surveys often place price as the fifth or sixth (out of ten) most important criterion on the list.[3]

Do I believe it?

Yes, with several caveats.

- ▶ Price is *never an issue* if you separate yourself from everyone else by presenting your sales value proposition.

- ▶ Price is *always an issue* if you look and sound like everyone else.

---

[3] Studies referenced in this publication include surveys from BDM News, HighTechCEO, and DigitalHatch, as well as information obtained through third-party research aggregators.

▶ Price is ***based on value and your ability to educate the prospect of that value.***

If, at the end of the sales cycle, you are still struggling with prospects on the price issue, more than likely you did not qualify them at the beginning of the cycle or educate them correctly on the value of your product or service. Usually when you lose a deal because of price, it means you failed to qualify the prospect correctly and did not position your offering's value so the prospect could *see* it (visual value).

Management *makes buying decisions* based on their impression of the vendor.

That's right, management teams do not sit around saying, *I need that product feature or this service report.* Instead, they make overall decisions based on how they feel about the vendor choices.

When reviewing vendors, management often says, *I like the firm. Something about them, I don't know what it is, but they seem to know our business needs and are specialists.*

That's why we try to avoid supervisors—they live for product or service minutia.

Creating the right image during your sales process will increase your sales negotiation success ratio regardless of the details or price. Creating a peer-to-peer relationship creates a *visual value* for prospects of why they should buy from you.

Visual value is the process of creating additional assets that unbalance the vendor's opinion of you and your competitors in your favor. It goes beyond the prospect thinking your service or support is great. *Visual value* is the overall impression a prospect has about your firm and why they should buy from you. It is not a variable they can hold, measure, or describe in detail.

Since supervisors can't touch, read, or describe visual value, they just ignore it.

Request for Proposal (RFP)

Depending on the product or service you sell and the size of the targeted companies you seek to penetrate, sometimes you may have to respond to a Request For Proposal (RFP). In some industries RFPs are *research projects* developed by supervisors who want to look busy to their bosses or collect pricing for next year's fiscal budget. Alternatively, RFPs may be tools used by development, manufacturing, and wholesaler prospects seeking external knowledge held by vendors on how to build or deliver their products or services internally.

Responding to an RFP is always a big debate.

Many of our consulting clients (both Fortune 1000 players and small businesses) confirm that regardless of the amount of time and effort they put into responding to RFPs, generally they win less than 20% of their submittals.

Many times when an RFP is received, both management and salespeople will project their hope, and not necessarily business logic, into their decision process of why they should respond to the inquiry. This sales projection is called the *RFP Rainbow Effect*, where salespeople and management are teased by the size of the projected revenue from the RFP regardless of the true percentage of closing opportunity that actually exists.

Remember, when you respond to an RFP, you are automatically positioning yourself as a vendor and not as a peer—thereby forcing yourself to be compared to other RFP respondents and your offering becomes a commodity—just like theirs.

When deciding to respond to an RFP, calculate your accurate chances to win, not the *rainbow* possibilities.

If you decide to respond to an RFP, here are some guidelines we use with our clients to become more successful.

RFP Success Guidelines

1. Respond to RFPs only when you have a prior relationship with the prospect.

2. Do not respond to blind RFPs where the vendor is not identified.

3. Determine your sales success potential before you submit. Do you normally sell to Fortune 5000 companies and the RFP is from a Fortune 50 prospect?

4. If possible, try to meet with the prospect before you submit the RFP, either through a general pre-RFP vendor discovery meeting or through a corporate conference call.

5. The key to winning RFPs is over-submitting. When RFP vendors are short-listed, it is because somewhere in the documentation their business value was communicated better than their competitors'. So, instead of submitting the minimum response that is requested in the RFP, supply multiple options to the buyer. Multiple payment pricing, extended service options, increase in product testing, more co-op dollars, or greater marketing support are examples of going beyond the RFP's basic requests. Many times, RFP reviewers will not let you communicate with them directly after the RFP

has been delivered (sometimes you can indirectly via e-mail). They do not want to tell you what your competitors have offered and ask you to reciprocate.

6. Communicate the full power of your sales value proposition by positioning your firm as a specialist and your competitors as generalists.

7. Audio record your response to the RFP.

8. Add a stand-alone CD with a five- to ten-minute audio message from your president or management team on why the vendor should select your firm over others.

9. Add a five- to ten-minute audio testimonial CD from your existing clients.

Case Study—Preparing a Management Proposal: Pricing

A few years ago, I was selling a business product with a services program to a Fortune 500 insurance company headquartered in the Northeast. The price for the package for the first year was $790,000. The prospect had short-listed my firm, along with one of my strongest competitors, and invited us both in to discuss our proposals. My competitor was also a Fortune 500 company but their first-year price came in at $450,000.

When I met with the management team after we were short-listed, they aggressively pursued me to explain why my price was $300,000, or 75%, higher than this well-known and established Fortune 500 player.

1.   I laid out my elevator pitch slowly and directly.

2.   I explained my sales value proposition again.

3.   I reconfirmed that we were specialists, **not** generalists.

4.   I focused on the pains they had described in our executive briefing meeting.

5.   I explained again how my product and service program would fix their pains and their increase profits.

6.   I focused on how selecting the wrong vendor because of price would affect their stated project outcome (consequence management). Additionally, that short-term savings could create a tidal wave of expense on the back end when they tried to fix the incorrectly selected vendor offering.

7.   Then, as a final shot across the table, I said, *To be honest, I would be nervous if you are getting a low-ball price. What do you think they are leaving out?*

Yes, I won the deal, even though we were 75% above our nearest competitor. Why? Because I created a value proposition that the client could not ignore. Even though there was a large difference in the price point, I forced the prospect to face reality and their business consequences.

Proposal Format

The following is a proven method I have used with clients and my account managers. It is based on the business case method taught in MBA graduate school to deduce business problems through a cause and effect relationship, using the primary and secondary discovery method process. It allows you to present your best positional understanding of your client's needs and how the acquisition of your product or service will increase corporate income and/or reduce corporate expenses.

You will use two binders. Binder No. 1 is provided to the decision maker and Binder No. 2 is provided to the lower-level supervisor who traditionally needs supporting documents. Binder No. 1 is called the "Executive Summary, Business Case Review" and Binder No. 2 is called the "Supporting Data."

Following is an outline of the contents for each binder. At the end of this chapter is an example of the format.

Binder No. 1

There are nine sections in this binder. Below are the sections, along with details on what each section consists of.

Section 1 – Executive Summary

The Executive Summary is composed of primary and secondary problems, as well as the problem resolution.

The Primary Problem is the pain identified by management. This should always be described as told by the prospect executive in charge. It should speak to the business case NOT the product or service features of what you're selling. For example, *the sales department has insufficient communication with inventory statuses; our payroll management process does not track 401k information; your salespeople do not use a contact manager program, etc.*

The Secondary Problem should describe the issues that are affected by the Primary Problem being present. For example, *sales are down, employee turnover is high, customer service expenses are up, etc.*

NOTE: The Secondary Problem is the reaction, fallout, or symptom of the Primary Problem. There can be more than one Secondary Problem. Try to have the Secondary Problem be an income or expense issue. Many people confuse the Primary Problem with the Secondary Problem.

Remember, the Primary Problem **causes** the Secondary Problem.

Next, the Problem Resolution is identified. For example, XYT Company is to acquire, install, and deploy a new racking system for the warehouse. This is the place where you identify whatever you are selling. Describe succinctly what product or service the firm will be buying from you.

Length: The Primary Problem, Secondary Problem(s), and Problem Resolution should consist of short summaries, usually two paragraphs per problem/resolution and placed together on one page.

Section 2 – Client Overview

In this section, you will describe the prospect's firm and department. Take information from actual company brochures, their web site, 10K etc. Describe business goals mentioned by senior decision makers or expressed in the 10K as issues that need to be resolved.

Length: This section should be approximately one page in length.

Section 3 – Primary Problem Detail

In this section, you should describe in detail the Primary Problem. Use information collected from the client. Since senior executives above the level you are dealing with may read this proposal, be cautious not to make the lower level contacts look bad.

Length: This section should be no more than two pages.

Section 4 – Secondary Problem Detail

In this section, you should describe the Secondary Problem(s) in detail, outlining how the Primary Problem is causing the Secondary Problem(s) to develop, i.e., sales are down (Secondary Problem) because the current sales team communication system is inadequate (Primary Problem) to keep the field sales staff knowledgeable, etc.

Length: This section should be no more than one page.

Section 5 – Problem Resolution Detail

You should list in detail your service or product methods that will resolve the Primary and Secondary Problems. Use bullets and be specific.

Length: This section should be no more than three pages.

Section 6 – Problem Resolution Examples

In this section, you should provide examples of case studies of companies that you have helped resolve similar issues. Do not just list references.

Length: This section should be no more than three pages.

Section 7 – Corporate Background

In this section, share your company information: contact data, size, employees, senior management executives by name and title, etc. In addition, name-drop references and their telephone numbers.

Length: This section should be no more than two pages.

Section 8 – Problem Resolution Investment

List the cost of purchase and what they get for their money. Discuss ROI minimally. (All of your competitors will discuss ROI.) Instead, focus on broader terms of total company income increase or total department expenses decrease if the Primary Problem is resolved. Do a potential five-year income increase forecast based on the investment.

Length: This section should be no more than two pages.

Section 9 – Conclusion

Write a succinct logical business case as to why your prospect should buy the service or product from you. Focus on how you will fix the Primary Problem, eliminate the Secondary Problem(s), and increase corporate income. Delicately discuss potential business consequences.

Length: This section should be no more than one page.

Binder No. 2

Binder No. 2 includes everything in Binder No. 1, plus supporting data. Assume that technical, administrative or operations managers will review this binder. List all of the information needed that is not listed anywhere else in the proposal, including:

- Project plans

- Product feature lists

- Manpower commitments required by client

- Technical specifications

- Deployment schedules

- Contract examples

- Payment terms

- Operation Manager's Bio

- Inventory requirements

- Key contact examples

Length: As many pages as needed.

Final Thought on Proposal Format

When submitting this kind of proposal, it is important to assume that everyone reading your presentation is not currently aware of what you do. So, the explanation of the business case needs to be succinct so that an outsider could pick up your presentation and understand who you are, what business problem you are trying to resolve, and what effect your problem resolution will have on the firm's income and expenses if they buy your offering.

Business case proposal methodology is a proven format that can make your firm stand out from the competitive environment, close deals with senior executives, and shorten your sales cycles.

Following are examples of the proposal format.

Section 1

(page 1 of 2)

Executive Summary

Primary Problem

Business Problem (pain) identified by management. This should always be described as told by the prospect executive in charge. It should speak to the business case NOT the product or service features of what you're selling. For example, the sales department has insufficient communication with inventory statuses; our payroll management process does not track 401K information; etc.

Secondary Problem

This area should describe the issues that are affected by the Primary Problem being present. For example, sales are down, employee turnover is high, customer service expenses are up, etc.

The secondary problem is always the reaction, fallout, or symptom of the Primary Problem. There can be more than one Secondary Problem. Try to have the Secondary Problem be an income or expense issue. Many people confuse the Primary Problem with the Secondary Problem. Remember, the Primary Problem causes the Secondary Problem.

Length: Keep these two sections short—maximum two paragraphs on a single page as shown.

Section 1
(page 2 of 2)

<u>Problem Resolution</u> XYT Company to acquire, install and deploy a new racking system for the warehouse (i.e., whatever you're selling). Describe succinctly what product or service the firm will be buying from you.

Length: Keep this short—two paragraphs, one page.

Section 2

<u>Client Overview</u>   Describe the prospect's firm and
department. Take information from actual
company brochures, their web site, 10K,
etc. Describe business goals mentioned by
senior decision makers or expressed in the
10K as issues that need to be resolved.

Length: One page.

Section 3

Primary Problem Detail   Describe in more detail the Primary
Problem. Use information and details
collected from the client. Since senior
managers above the level you are
dealing with may read this proposal, be
cautious not to make the lower level
contacts look bad.

Length: No more than two pages.

Section 4

Secondary Problem Detail

Describe the Secondary Problem(s) in detail, outlining how the Primary Problem is causing the Secondary Problem(s) to develop, i.e., sales are down (Secondary Problem) because the current sales team communication system is inadequate (Primary Problem) to keep the field sales staff knowledgeable, etc.

Length: No more than one page.

Section 5

Problem Resolution Detail   Listed in detail your service or
product methods that will resolve
the Primary and Secondary
Problems. Use bullets and be
specific.

Length: No more than three pages.

Section 6

Problem Resolution Examples   List examples of case studies
of companies that you helped
resolve similar issues. Do not
just list references.

Length: No more than three pages.

Section 7

<u>Corporate Background</u> List your company information: contact data, size, employees, senior management executives by name and title, etc. In addition, name drop references and their telephone numbers.

Length: No more than two pages.

Section 8

<u>Problem Resolution Investment</u>

List the cost of purchase and what they get for their money. Discuss ROI minimally. (All of your competitors will discuss ROI.) Instead, focus on broader terms of total company income increase or total department expenses decrease if the Primary Problem is resolved. Do a potential five-year income increase forecast based on the investment.

Length: No more than two pages.

Section 9

<u>Conclusion</u>

Write a succinct logical business case as to why your prospect should buy the service/product from you, focusing on how you will fix the Primary Problem, eliminate the Secondary Problem, and increase corporate income. Cover potential business consequences.

Length: One page only.

Chapter 8
Preparing a Management Proposal That Works

Review and Exercises

1. Next time you are in an executive's office, observe the surroundings and make mental notes. Try to quickly determine whether the executive is a risk taker or a conservative decision maker. You can also practice this by going into your manager's office and trying to assess him or her using these same techniques.

2. Take one of your existing proposals and convert it to the format provided in this chapter. This will help you gather your thoughts for the next proposal that you need to prepare.

3. Create a list of potential business consequences that could happen to your prospect if they don't buy or they buy from the wrong vendor. Use the list as a sales cycle tool to manage communication with prospects both verbally as well as through written proposals.

Chapter 8
Preparing a Management Proposal That Works

Chapter 9

Negotiating With Management

After reading this chapter, you will know:

- Who should you negotiate with

- What you should negotiate

- How to negotiate from value, not win-win

- What types of personalities you will be negotiating with

- How to use concession management

- How to control your emotions during the negotiation process

Negotiation is the transfer of value from one person to another. To make negotiation successful with management, it must be a planned process, not a haphazard interaction. The value communicated by each participant should include reasons why this transfer of value should take place.

When negotiating with management for a product or service deal, often you are *not* in the room when the deal is finalized. Usually it is a series of meetings, demos, proposals, and discussions used as a driver to close deals. Sometimes your negotiation tactics and strategies are communicated by your contact to a corporate steering committee or executive board for final approval.

Due to this multi-layered decision process, it is important to keep negotiating throughout your sales cycle to increase your product and service sales success.

Negotiation training for executives is one of the most popular business courses today. Executives know it is to their advantage to negotiate at the end of the month or at the end of the business quarter with a salesperson because they can get better price concessions.

Management buyers know if they tell you they are going to buy your product or service, you will commit this to your sales forecast or contact manager system. Then they play poker with you on pricing by telling you that they have changed their mind. They recognize that once you have committed to your management it is a done deal, you (and your sales management team) will now be forced by the buyer to save the deal by reacting to their requested concessions.

In most cases, management buyers are more educated on negotiation techniques than the salespeople who call on them. This education imbalance threatens every sales opportunity.

So, before we get into the techniques of negotiating with management, first let's review how management buys. From there, you can analyze what you need to say and do to induce the prospect to take an action step. Since planning is an important part of any negotiation process, we will build a prototype model based on three elements. Each of these elements will affect your ability to close more deals.

- Who should you negotiate with?

- What should you negotiate?

- How do you negotiate from value, not win-win?

Who Should You Negotiate With?

If you are looking to increase your success selling more products and services, then you must negotiate *only* with management. It is tempting to negotiate with supervisors, but the moment you do this, you will pull yourself into commodity. Supervisors select products and services based on feature, function, or price. Negotiating with supervisors is always a difficult place to be because there will always be another vendor whose product or service appears to be better or their company is more recognizable, which ends up blurring your business value.

When a supervisor starts to negotiate with you, your response to their inquiry sets the pattern of what they expect and what you must give.

Let me repeat that.

If you respond to the supervisor's negotiation inquiries, you are setting yourself up for failure because you are now acting like a vendor and you will be forced to offer and counteroffer based on what other competitors are doing, not on your business value.

As discussed earlier, selling (or negotiating) below the title of director usually means you are perceived to be a commodity—thus your negotiations will be based on price only.

To avoid this, don't negotiate with them. Now, wait— I didn't say *don't* negotiate. I just said don't negotiate with *supervisors*. You should only negotiate with *management*.

John Kennedy once said, "Let us never negotiate out of fear. But let's never fear to negotiate." So, negotiations with management are sequential planned processes, not haphazard interactions.

To be successful in selling to management, negotiation techniques should be used throughout your entire sales cycle, not just at the end.

What Should You Negotiate?

If you are selling to management, regardless of what you sell, their business needs force them to look at what you sell from only *three* perspectives.

1. How your product or service will help them increase income (or revenue) in their business

2. How your product or service will decrease their business operation costs

3. How your product or service will manage their business risks

They are not buying bicycle parts, software, wholesale furniture, strategy services, staffing, or a fleet of new corporate cars. **Management buys the results that your product or service delivers** and the results must directly increase their business success. Based on this approach, never negotiate the features or functions you have or don't have; instead, <u>negotiate the value it delivers</u>.

In our world of ever-changing product and service development, someone is always building a superior mousetrap.

How do you create value for your product or service?

1. **Categorize and box all competitors as generalists and your firm as a specialist. Then discuss the competition as a category.** This establishes a more professional benchmark when you negotiate because you don't sell negatively by mentioning a competitor directly but rather talk about the category they reside in—generalists.

2. When positioning your firm as a specialist, you add value. Management likes to buy from specialists, not generalists, and will pay a premium if you create the right *visual brochure* in their head.

It is important to remember that when negotiating with management, you do not have a *relationship* until after they buy the first time. I know the term *relationship sales* is used widely and often by both salespeople and sales management, but you don't have a relationship just because prospects let you buy them lunch, meet with you in their office, or accept your phone calls.

During the negotiation process the term *relationship* may be used by the prospect as a technique to induce you to reduce your price. Often they will say, *Work with us on price now and we can build a long-term relationship with your firm.*

Evidence today indicates there is no guarantee that cutting your price is going to give you more than one sale.[4] And once you cut your price, you are now positioning yourself in the buyer's mind as a commodity that can be managed on future price negotiations. All price concessions set the stage for future concessions.

Remember, your first sale to a new prospect is a *transactional sale*. If you believe that your first sale is going to turn into repetitive future sales and a business relationship, all you are really doing is projecting your business needs onto the buyer.

Why is this?

Because when you sell to management, you have three stages of the sale. They are:

1. **The Pre-Sales Cycle** where you educate the buyer why they should buy from you and how your business value makes your firm different.

2. **The Sales Cycle** where the prospect buys based on the value you said you would deliver.

---

[4] Studies referenced in this publication include surveys from BDM News, HighTechCEO, and DigitalHatch, as well as information obtained through third-party research aggregators.

3. **The Post-Sales Cycle** where the prospect determines if your product or service delivers the value you said it could deliver during the pre-sales cycle.

If they believe that your value as discussed in pre-sales is delivered in the post-sales cycle, then they will decide to start a relationship and buy from you again.

When selling to management, relationship sales start after the second sale. Don't be misled by buyers who use the term *relationship* when negotiating. It's a tool to get you to drop your price.

▶ **Transactional sales** are sales generated from prospects who have a short-term need.

▶ **Relationship sales** are sales from prospects who have a long-term need and have already bought from you at least once.

The goal is to turn all transactional sales (your first sales) into relationship sales (subsequent sales).

Six Steps In Relationship Sales

2nd Purchase - Relationship Starts	6
Post-Sales Value Proven	5
1st Purchase - Transactional Sale	4
Value Belief Starts	3
Value Introduced	2
Pre-Sale Introduction	1

Figure 14. *Six Steps In Relationship Sales.* This figure shows the progress of the sales cycle from pre-sales to the second sale.

How to Negotiate From Value, Not Win-Win

Always negotiate on the business value of what you sell, not the product, service, features, or functions.

The concept of win-win has been around a long time, but it implies that all things are equal. **There is nothing equal in negotiation with management.**

Never negotiate a win-win scenario. Instead, negotiate a value purchase. Executives buy value that produces results. Many times when you're negotiating with a prospect, you may be competing against some other asset investment the prospect is considering rather than a direct competitor of the product or service you sell.

▶ Is the management prospect weighing a
decision to buy a trainload of raw steel or a new
plant assembly machine against your product or
service?

▶ Is the prospect contemplating hiring more
salespeople or buying your marketing services?

You have no idea, so you must negotiate from your
own position of strength, which is business value.

When you use a win-win scenario, you fall into the
gamut of your direct competitors and their
concessions or negotiation give backs and the prospect
expects you to respond accordingly. Using a win-win
scenario pulls you down into the commodity zone.
Value allows you to negotiate what you offer, not what
your competitors give away. **If you act like your
competitor, then you must give the discounts they
give.**

Negotiation Personality Types

The Study of Enneagram. When negotiating with
management prospects, you can increase your sales
success by understanding their personality type. The
study of Enneagram can be traced back to before 2000
B.C. and is of Greek origin. It identifies nine different
patterns of personality that intersect and can be used
as a logical process to understand yourself and others

during negotiations. Understanding these personality types will allow you to adjust your negotiation tactics and techniques.

To make it easier, we have placed the most common observations of the nine personality types into three broad categories to help you understand how to negotiate and present your business value to each buyer.

Abstract Buyers. Usually they are right-brain, emotional, and creative types who use intuitive thought to make business decisions. More times than not, they have a marketing education, design, or artistic background, and often are left-handed.

Titles often held by this personality are:

- Director of Design

- Vice President of Marketing

- Director of Entertainment

- General Manager of Human Resources

When negotiating with this type of personality, use client testimonials, discuss how the product or service you sell can be used long-term, and discuss how you are seeking a strategic partnership and will want their input.

Example Buyers. This type of management buyer looks at decisions from multiple perspectives and weighs visual evidence as a technique to buy. They often think in terms of examples. Their university education is often business management or accounting. Titles often held by this personality are:

- Chief Operating Officer

- President

- General Manager

- Chief Executive Officer

- Vice President of Sales

When negotiating with this type of personality, use written case studies, show company logos of your existing clients or strategic partners, and use overhead presentations (minimally) with visual examples of how you can fix their business needs. This type of buyer likes the written word.

Analytical/Logical Buyers. This type of management buyer often has a mathematical, engineering, or science education. Their thought process for buying is a structured, detailed analysis of why they should buy. When negotiating with this type of buyer, give detailed numbers, facts, and financial information. They like percent-driven data and third-party endorsements from independent research groups.

Titles often held by this personality are:

- Vice President of Construction

- Chief Buyer

- Chief Information Officer

- Chief Financial Officer

- Vice President of Engineering

- Vice President of Operations

How to Use Concession Management When Negotiating

Regardless of the Enneagram personality type you are negotiating with, one of the most effective business tools you can use to create value and close deals is a concession list. A **concession list** is a sales tool that helps guide you through the negotiation process to help control your emotions during tense conversations and to communicate your business value to executives you are working with.

Management buyers are just like you and I. They need to feel they negotiated a good deal. It does not matter if they are buying a $200 million corporate office building, a $100,000 tractor, or a $30,000 custom software module. Everyone has an intrinsic need to feel that he negotiated well and bought at a good price. It is the buyer's job to get the lowest price (in his mind) and it is your job, as a professional salesperson, to get the highest price.

To some degree, all salespeople develop a mental concession list in their minds when they are trying to negotiate a deal to close. The best way to develop this is to use a written concession list rather than relying on your memory. It keeps you focused and prevents you from changing your mind midway through the negotiation process. Sometimes the concession list is recommended or approved by your boss as tools you can use to close the deal. Regardless, always use a written concession list as a business sales tool to sell more.

Negotiating terms of a purchase is a psychological and financial poker game. By creating a written concession list, you decide ahead of time what you will give and what you will ask for when negotiating with management. When selling to management, you must give them the illusion that you will give them a good deal. You must give them something to feed their psychological need.

A concession list is a psychological tool, so always use a written concession list each time you negotiate.

Guidelines to Create a Concession List

1. Determine what type of Enneagram personality you think you are going to negotiate with.

2. Try to create a list of concessions based on the personality of the buyer.

3. List on paper the concessions you will give.

4. List the concessions you think the prospect will ask for.

5. Divide all of the concessions into five separate categories identified as **A, B, C, D** and **E**.

6. Category A contains items you will give to the buyer easily after they ask.

7. Category B contains items the management buyer must pull away from you and negotiate for.

8. Category C contains items you will not give under any circumstances.

9. Category D contains items you are going to ask the prospect for (like testimonials or case studies)

10. Category E contains the consequences you will tell them could happen if the prospect does not buy from you.

The goal for all concession management is to control the prospect's wants with your needs and fill their psychological need to believe they received a good deal.

- Never give concessions that you hope to make up on the next deal.

- Never give price concessions on the first request. The buyer's job is to buy at the lowest price; your job is to sell at the highest price.

Emotion Management When Negotiating

As a salesperson you have a tendency to project your business needs onto the prospect when you negotiate. This projection during negotiation comes out as emotion. When negotiating with a management buyer, the four needs you must deal with are:

1. Your need to sell or hit your assigned sales quota or target

2. Your need to have more money or increase your commission

3. Your need to sell a deal to keep your job or make your boss happy

4. Your need to satisfy your ego that you are better at negotiating than other salespeople and your prospect

But the management buyer does not care about your needs. She only cares about hers. If you can manage your emotions during the negotiation, you can increase your closing ratio dramatically.

Control your emotions during negotiation by following these guidelines:

- Before you start negotiating with a prospect, **write down the top ten sales objections you expect them to ask and your responses**. This will prepare you for tough questions and will keep your emotions invisible.

- Carry a prop (pad of paper, pen, etc.). When a prospect says something that upsets you, tighten the prop to displace your emotion into the object.

- Anytime a prospect asks you unreasonable or difficult questions, pause and count to ten

silently, then lean forward and respond. By
hesitating and counting to ten, you allow your
heart rate to slow down and you gain control of
your emotions.

- Never take prospect comments or requests
  personally, even if they make it personal. This is
  the *game of business*. Always ask the prospect why
  it is important to receive their concession. This
  will give you time to collect yourself and slow
  down the negotiation process and your
  immediate reaction.

Controlling your emotions is controlling the sale.

Eight Steps to Force Prospects to Prove They Are Qualified Buyers During Negotiation

1. When negotiating with a prospect over a
   difficult concession item, always table the issue
   and try to move on to other items. If the buyer
   only focuses on that one item he may not be
   ready to buy.

2. After you have agreed to a major concession,
   immediately put the prospect on a timetable to
   accept the deal or not.

3. Always ask the prospect if he or she is the one who will sign the contract or purchase order.

4. When you have gone through all of the items under your Category A concession list, immediately ask for the purchase order.

5. If you get a serious impasse when negotiating a specific item that is on your Category C concession list, tell the prospect you need to regroup with your management team to discuss, but also ask to set up another meeting with them at a later date. If he is a qualified buyer, he will take an action step with you during the sales cycle and make a new meeting.

6. Tell the buyer that your management team only allows you to negotiate with the person who signs the contract. If they cannot sign the agreement personally but they go get the person who does sign, then you have closed the deal. This method is called *the walk*.

7. When the prospect asks for a concession, you should ask them for something from Category D.

8. When the prospect asks for a concession from Category C, you should discuss a business consequence from Category E.

Fifteen Tactical and Strategic Steps to Use When Negotiating

1. Plan your negotiation meeting. Never shoot from the hip.

2. Always start talking about your business value *before* you start negotiating terms.

3. Before the negotiations start get your prospect to acknowledge your product or service value. (This is visual value.)

4. Immediately hesitate on the first concession the prospect asks for. Studies show that the longer it takes for a buyer to get a concession (even concession items in Category A), the greater they value them.

5. Practice and role-play with your office colleagues about what you are going to say. **Most salespeople never role-play negotiations.** Practice helps.

6. Never give a client a concession unless they give something in return. Always ask for something (e.g., a testimonial, case study, anything that will help subliminally teach the prospect that when they ask for something, you will also ask for something.)

7. Always write down every discussed concession. Keep specific details ready to discuss as the negotiation progresses.

8. Use silence as a negotiation tool when unreasonable things are asked for. The act of hesitation creates psychological pressure on the prospect and forces them to rethink their request.

9. Never let a prospect bully you about deadlines. More times than not, this is a negotiation tactic.

10. Never be the bad person in the room. If a prospect does not like your terms, your contract, or the concession you are offering, third-party the concession out of the room— blame your corporate office, your president, your sales manager, your legal department—but don't have the prospect direct their frustration at you.

11. When a prospect tells you about her business needs, always agree with her that it is important. Agreeing is not *accepting*, but it does show peer-to-peer respect.

12. When asked for a price concession, give something of greater value without dropping your price.

13. When negotiating across a conference table or an executive's desk, adjust your body position to the discussion. When the prospect asks for a concession, lean back in your chair. When you ask for a concession, lean forward.

14. If possible, never e-mail a proposal to a senior executive. E-mail has negatively affected the sales closing ratio of many salespeople. You send the proposal to the prospect and then it disappears. Always try to hand deliver the proposal to the prospect so you can discuss the details of its contents in person.

15. Ask the prospect, *What does my firm need to do to get your business?* Once you hear their requests, tell the prospect how you feel about their terms. **Peers ask why and discuss—vendors argue and get frustrated.**

Seven Questions You Must Answer to Close Any Deal

Negotiating with management requires you to use some or all of the techniques described in this course. However, to close any opportunity, regardless of whether it is large or small, new or existing, you must know the answers to the following seven questions. If you do not know these answers or you provide a generic response for each, your ability to negotiate and close deals will be hampered.

1. Why would the prospect buy from you? What's their business pain?

2. Why would you lose the deal?

3. What are the top ten expected sales objections you anticipate to hear from the decision-making team?

4. What is the political environment of the decision?

5. What does your firm have to do to close this sale and to meet the prospect's personal and business needs?

6. What are the business consequences that the prospect is exposed to if they do not buy from you or from another competitor whose product or service does not fix their business pain?

7. What is their stated budget for your product or service?

The correct answers to these seven questions will be your gateway to better negotiations and an increase of sales. Many sales methods today want you to over-complicate your sales cycle, but if you know the right answers to these seven questions, you can sell anybody anything.

Client Negotiation Form

Client Name_____
Date _____

Client Contact_____ Title_____

Account Manager_____

1.   Why will the management prospect buy from us? What's their business pain?_____
_____

2.   Why will we lose the deal? _____
_____

3.   What are the top ten expected sales objections we anticipate to hear from the decision-making team? _____
_____
_____

4.   What is the political environment of the decision? _____
_____

5.   What does your firm have to do to close this sale and to meet the prospect's personal and business needs? _____
_____

6.   What are the business consequences that the prospect is exposed to if they do not buy at all, or they buy from another competitor whose product or service does not fix their business pain? _____
_____

7.   What is their stated budget for your product or service?_____
_____

Figure 15.   *Client Negotiation Form.* Use this form to develop your concession list.

Case Study—Negotiating

I was working with a firm that sold services and products to privately held companies that were often family run businesses. The average sale was $50,000.We had a lot of competition in the marketplace, and price points were dropping in the industry to a commodity level.

When negotiating with the senior management teams of these firms, family members displayed or voiced financial, emotional, and ego issues every time I met with them.

Prior to my joining the firm, the sales team had grown accustomed to going in and immediately dropping their price whenever the prospects asked for a discount, which caused the firm to lose gross margin and in some cases be perceived to be a commodity like everyone else.

To change this process, we created a concession list, raised the price of the service offering and developed a sales value proposition as a business specialist who fixes management problems and manages business consequences. When the prospects asked for a discount, we gave them certain items from our predetermined concession list. By raising our prices and managing their discount requests through our concession list, we actually increased the average sale's gross margin and closing ratio.

Why? Because by changing the perceptions of the offering value (using the SVP), communicating that we could control business consequences (psychological ROI), and giving the prospect something of value when they asked for a discount (concession list), we helped the prospect see our value.

Chapter 9
Negotiating With Management

Review and Exercises

1. Prepare a Client Negotiation Form for one of the deals you are currently working on. If there are no deals in progress, prepare the form based on a prospect you would like to meet and present to.

2. Write down the top ten sales objections you receive or expect a prospect to ask, then write down your responses. Try to detach yourself from the responses and see if you can visualize being in the prospect's shoes. This is designed to help you become objective and understand how to relate to the prospect on a peer-to-peer level.

3. Develop a concession list. Segment each product or service that you offer and make a list of items you would automatically give, those items that the prospect has to ask for, and those items that you will never provide. Separate your concessions into Categories A, B, C, D and E.

Chapter 9
Negotiating With Management

Chapter 10

Selling to Targeted Key or Major Accounts

After reading this chapter, you will know:

- How to map your key account territory

- How to penetrate and manage key accounts

- How to use the Key Account Territory Success Pyramid Management to help you forecast more accurately and manage your sales pipeline more efficiently

- What steps you should use to develop the lifetime value of key accounts

- How to use the Key Account Action Wheel to shorten your sales cycle

- How to manage sales cycle steps before, during, and after the targeted key account sale.

When selling to major and targeted key accounts, there are many misperceptions promulgated by those who believe that penetrating the no-talk zone of management is based on being more visible in the account, taking the prospect to lunch, and hoping to be on the vendor's short list. But selling to key accounts is a *planned* process.

Selling to management of key accounts requires you to focus on managing your assigned territory correctly and understanding what management buys. Time management is important when selling to key accounts.

Three specific areas of managing key accounts are:

1. Mapping your key account territory

2. Mapping individual accounts

3. Penetrating key accounts

Mapping Your Key Account Territory

One of the decisions all salespeople need to make, specifically major account salespeople, is how to manage one's sales territory for maximum market potential and sales quota success.

When you are assigned key accounts, the time to sell each one is often disproportionate to other territory assignments and sales opportunities that you may be required to respond to.

To successfully sell to key accounts, you must manage your assigned sales territory effectively. **The sales**

paradigm is that the buying cycle and the selling cycle are never the same. So, unless your firm gives you two or more years to sell your assigned sales quota, you need to determine which accounts you should focus on to sell more and keep your job.

Mapping Individual Accounts

The *Territory Success Pyramid* is one business tool you can use to help manage the sales paradigm. The Territory Success Pyramid is a simple process that works with any key account and helps to improve your time management.

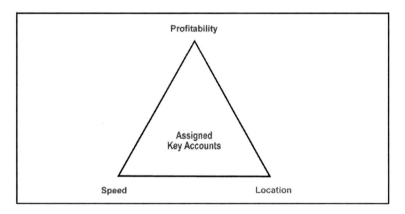

Figure 16.   *Territory Success Pyramid.*

Take each key account you are working on or have been assigned to and grade each account in the three categories of **Speed**, **Profitability**, and **Location**.

- **Speed** measures the length of time it will take you to close the account

- **Location** measures the distance you must travel to get to a key account from your location of departure

- **Profitability** measures the size of the gross margin or gross revenue of the key account opportunity you are trying to sell

Now grade each account either "A", "B" or "C."

- "A" is an opportunity that is better than most accounts because it is geographically close or financially larger than your average deal.

- "B" is an opportunity that is average in its potential or geographically not too far away

- "C" is an opportunity that is below average in its potential or is geographically distant

For example, let's assume, your average key account sale is worth $100,000, takes six months to close, and you live in Atlanta, Georgia. The key account you are reviewing is called Smith, Inc. The sales opportunity is worth $800,000; will take eight months to close; and is located in Miami, Florida. You would code this opportunity as follows:

> **Speed:** C – This account will take longer than your average six-month sales cycle.
>
> **Location:** B – This account is in your time zone and not too far away geographically.
>
> **Profitability:** A – The dollar value of this account is higher than your average sale.
>
> Smith Inc. key account status is a **CBA.**

Once you code all of your top key accounts, focus on all of the accounts with the most As first, then the Bs, and then the Cs. If an account is **AAB,** it is given a higher priority than an account with a status of **ABB.**

This is a quick method to determine where you should focus your time and energy. It is not a perfect process, because there are always business anomalies. Your boss might say, *go sell that account,* and it might be an account with a CCC classification that has a long sales cycle, a small dollar value, and is geographically isolated from where you work. However, it might be an important reference for your company. Your boss told you do it, so it's important.

Use the Territory Success Pyramid once a week and you will improve your time management.

Penetrating Key or Major Accounts

Spidering Key Accounts. Selling to targeted or key accounts takes time and effort to maximize your sales penetration potential. One way to do this is by using a process we call *spidering*. Spidering is a process by which you penetrate a key account with multiple contacts.

When trying to sell to a specific large corporate account, most salespeople select one or two entry points as a model to sell. *This is an incorrect process.* If you are positioning yourself as a peer in the boardroom instead of a vendor in the hallway, you can elevate your product or service presentation goals to multiple department heads regardless of what you sell. If you are selling like a vendor based on feature or function strength, then your key account entry point may be limited to one corporate contact.

Four Guidelines to Spidering Key Accounts

1. Understand what your key account penetration opportunities are. Develop an organizational chart for the key account you are targeting. This will help you identify who to talk with, where they fit in the decision-making process, and

who else you should seek to maximize your
sales opportunities.

2. Pick five to seven entry points by title in
   different divisions, preferably at the title of VP
   and above.

3. Create a sales value proposition on the product
   or service for each of the targeted contact
   points you are seeking to spider into.

4. Contact each prospect in your targeted group
   within five days of each other.

Understanding that not all prospects talk to (or
welcome) vendors in the beginning of a sales cycle and
all prospects make different buying decisions based on
their priorities, not yours, is the key to making the
spider model work.

By spidering into multiple key contacts at the same
time in a company, you are casting a wide net based on
your sales value proposition to see which key account
contact is going to take an action step with you and
move into a sales cycle.

Follow the path of interest even if more than one
prospect moves you forward during the sales cycle.
Having multiple corporate management team
members interested in your product or service is not a
bad thing.

When trying to sell to management, spider in and don't count on one contact being your doorway to a sale.

Key accounts do not make business purchases through an educated program where all decision makers and their advisors move (or roll) at the same speed during the investigative process. We refer to this philosophy of same buying timeline as *the spoke and wheel model* of buyers. There is an assumption that all levels of management and their staffs roll together like a wheel and come to a group conclusion together (even when there is a company-imposed buying deadline). However, this is incorrect.

Based on their interests, education levels, time available, and business priorities, multiple buying groups act as individuals and make decisions at their own pace.

At times, you may have to meet and educate other staff types on the value of your product and service before you are allowed to get to higher levels of management. Although this is not a preferred method of selling, it is sometimes the reality of selling to large key accounts depending on what you sell.

When selling to key accounts, there are four key account contact types that need to be managed. We use the *Major Account Action Plan (MAAP) wheel* to identify each type. (See Figure 17) They are:

- Quadrant 1—Product or Service, Feature or Function Contacts

- Quadrant 2—Product or Service Value Contacts

- Quadrant 3—Product or Service Operational Pain Management Contacts

- Quadrant 4—Product or Service Economic Pain Management Contacts

Quadrant 1—Product or Service Feature or Function Contacts. This group usually includes low-level managers, supervisors, or analyst-types who make judgments about your product or service based on its price, features, or functions and how it will personally affect their jobs.

Quadrant 2—Product or Service Value Contacts. This group includes supervisors who may hold the title of director and are usually decision advisors and sometimes decision makers. These prospects are focused on the functions or features of what you sell and how it will affect their individual department vertically.

Quadrant 3—Product or Service Operational Pain Management Contacts. This group includes management executives who often hold titles of vice president of marketing, vice president of engineering, vice president of operations, and vice president of information systems and are generally classified as decisions makers focused on their department horizontally and how your product or service will affect their success operationally.

Quadrant 4—Product or Service Economic Pain Management Contacts. This group includes senior executives who are decision makers holding titles such as general manager, chief financial officer, chief operating officer, chief executive officer, or president. They focus on the overall economic impact of your product or service.

Major Account Action Plan Wheel

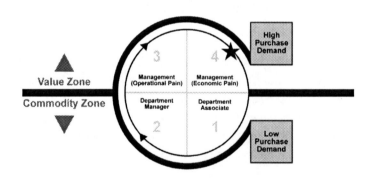

Figure 17.   ***Major Account Action Plan (MAAP).*** This chart illustrates various entry points and identifies how each entry point affects the length of your sales cycle.

Selling to Decision Makers and Influencers at the Same Time

We developed the MAAP wheel as a tool to help salespeople understand categories of key account buyers and the steps necessary to keep forward momentum in the sales cycle. As you look at the MAAP wheel, the goal is to bypass the entry points of Quadrants 1 and 2 and focus on Quadrants 3 and 4. Quadrants 1 and 2 are commodity quadrants and your business value will be diminished. Quadrants 3 and 4 are the value quadrants and your business value will be believed.

If you are spidering into an account, the best place to enter simultaneously is within Quadrants 3 and 4, contacting multiple key entry points at the same time. When you penetrate a key account, there are prospects who pull you forward in your sales cycle and those who hold you back. The contacts who pull you forward are called *leaders* and the contacts who hold you back are called *laggers*.

To successfully move forward in your sales cycle, you need to classify the key account contacts you have made and decide if they are leaders or laggers.

If they are laggers, you can sub-segment these contacts into four separate categories. These four categories are:

1. **Political Laggers**—They focus on existing vendor relationships and may be friends with your competitors.

2. **Ego Laggers**—They often feel insecure in their jobs and your product or service may threaten their stability. Alternatively, they may think they can get a better deal on what you sell from someone else or by producing it internally.

3. **Technical Laggers**—They are business contacts who focus on technical specifications and deliverables based on the type of product and service you supply.

4. **Financial Laggers**—They focus on the pricing minutia of your product or service and many times subliminally evaluate the cost of your product or service based on how much they are paid annually (in relation to what you are tying to sell) or on how much they personally can afford.

To move forward in your key account MAAP in a clockwise motion, it is critical to understand which category your lagger comes from so you can plot your next strategic move.

A key account sale, like all professional sales, involves a premeditated process of thought, planning, and action. **Manage laggers; hunt for leaders.**

Using the Pursuit Sales Team Model to Increase Key Account Revenue

One way for product and service companies to increase revenue is by developing *pursuit sales teams* for key or targeted major accounts. The pursuit sales team model uses your firm's collective sales, marketing, and strategic knowledge to analyze key selling opportunities and determine the appropriate way to premeditatedly sell to targeted accounts. It is a strategic process that focuses on generating specific revenue from one company based on a premeditated selling process. Often used for large national and international company sales, its methodology also holds well for smaller companies. Here are seven steps to deploy a pursuit sales team.

1. **Select pursuit sales team members.**
   The selection of a key account pursuit sales team is the basic foundation of any major account success. Questions will be raised such as:

   o Should an account manager who is located within the geography of the key

account's corporate headquarters be part
of the team?

o Should company marketing and
operations personnel be included on the
pursuit sales team?

o Does your vice president of sales have to
be part of the pursuit sales team?

Selling in this team environment requires people
to set aside their egos, and sometimes titles, to
determine the best distribution of talent to help
your firm sell to your targeted accounts. Always
pick skilled people from operations, sales,
engineering, and management to form a nucleus
of your pursuit sales team.

2. **Develop the pursuit sales team's
preliminary strategy.**
Selling to targeted accounts requires an
individualized sales approach that starts as a
perception of the prospect's business needs and
ends with their actual needs, which are
determined in a later phase. Using a cookie-
cutter approach based on similar key accounts
experiences or previous sales into this existing
account will only minimize your success. When
selling to targeted accounts, each prospect has
his/her own acceptance criteria that can change
deal by deal. Custom-fit your preliminary sales

strategy to what you are trying to sell, the firm
you are selling to, and the executive who signs
the purchase order or contract.

3. **Identify your firm's sales value proposition.**
You must identify why a prospect should buy
from you. You need a better answer than: *We
have the most experienced practice managers* or *We are
concerned about customer service*, because answers
like these sound like vanilla ice cream. To sell to
key accounts, you must know why they will buy
from you instead of your competitors.

4. **Identify why you may not succeed at selling
to the targeted account.**
Of course you want to believe that when a key
account is presented a compelling reason to buy
your product or service, there is a logical reason
for them not to buy it. But selling to key
accounts is not always a logical process. It
requires a premeditated sales process to help
you limit sales process bottlenecks.
Management never buys on price, features, or
functions. Management always buys on
impression. During your Phase 1 Pre-sales
Strategy, analyze why you might not sell the key
account and manage the sales objections *before*
they happen.

5. **Identify key account contacts to be targeted.**

   As I mentioned before, it is common for key account sales methods to focus on one contact entry point. This is a serious mistake. When trying to sell to strategic accounts through a pursuit sales team process, always make multiple management contacts at the same time to increase your odds of penetration. Also determine who will contact which prospect. When launching into a new account, seek parallel sales paths to maximize your success. Relying on one contact minimizes your closing opportunities.

6. **Plan your meeting and develop talking points.**

   The use of a pursuit sales team model requires the development of specific tactical talking points for all members of the sales team to use in harmony. Have you ever sat in a key account sales meeting with management prospects and one of your team members says the wrong thing? This usually happens because people have an innate need to feel as though they contributed to the sales process. When team members are not prepped for the meeting, they can respond inadvertently and say the wrong thing. When focusing on key accounts, *always* distribute typed talking points for all team members to plan what should be said and what should *not* be said.

7. **Identify contact methods that will be used to reach targeted key contacts on the first introduction.**
Now that you have developed your team pre-strategy, created talking points, and identified your entry positions, you must decide how your first foray into the key account will be accomplished. Will it be a cold call or an introduction by a business partner? Will you network or are you going to have a lower-level manager introduce you? Each one of these processes has its impact on later sales steps and needs to be weighed carefully. Management paints visual brochures about you and your firm based on what words you use and how they are introduced the first time. So, always paint your visual brochure in a positive way on the first contact. It could be your last contact.

Pursuit Sales Team Process

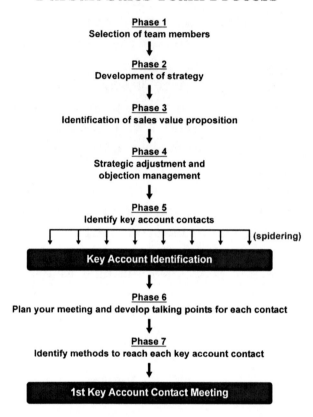

Phase 1
Selection of team members
↓
Phase 2
Development of strategy
↓
Phase 3
Identification of sales value proposition
↓
Phase 4
Strategic adjustment and
objection management
↓
Phase 5
Identify key account contacts
↓ ↓ ↓ ↓ ↓ ↓ ↓ ↓ (spidering)
Key Account Identification
↓
Phase 6
Plan your meeting and develop talking points for each contact
↓
Phase 7
Identify methods to reach each key account contact
↓
1st Key Account Contact Meeting

Figure 18. ***Pursuit Sales Team Process.*** This illustration shows the progress of developing the pursuit sales team leading up to the first meeting.

Use the Pursuit Sales Team sales process to create an outbound premeditated selling process for targeted key accounts.

Review and Exercises

1. Make a list of your current opportunities. Rate them according to Speed, Location, and Profitability. As are opportunities that are better than most, Bs are average opportunities, and Cs are below-average opportunities.

2. Review your current key account sales opportunities. Decide what quadrant your contacts are in. If you are in the commodity zone, determine if you are working with a leader or a lagger. If you are working with a lagger, determine which type of lagger they are and plot your plan of action to move forward accordingly.

3. To help develop spidering techniques, list a key account that you are currently trying to contact.

    a. Make two columns and title them "Current Contacts" and "Potential Contacts." Under Current Contacts, list the names and titles of the contacts you have attempted to meet. Under Potential Contacts, list five to seven management contacts that are listed in the company's organizational chart with the title of VP or above. This can usually be found on the corporate web site under management.

b. Create a sales value proposition on the product or service for each of the targeted contact points you are seeking to spider into.

c. Contact each prospect under Potential Contacts within five days of each other.

Chapter 11

Managing Your Sales Cycle and Forecasting

After reading this chapter, you will know:

- How to benefit from a Sales Action Plan (SAP)

- How to benefit from a Marketing Action Plan (MAP)

- How to manage your sales cycle and forecast more accurately

- How to use a Major Account Action Plan (MAAP) format to lay out your management sales approach

- What a Date Management Plan is and how you can use it to increase your sales efficiency

SAP and MAP Management

One of the most effective tools for personal sales management is called a *Sales Action Plan* (SAP). Once a month, you evaluate each client in your sales pipeline that is forecast to close that month and develop a

SAP—a detailed list of dates and actions required to close business that month.

Similarly, you use a *Marketing Action Plan* (MAP) to plan marketing steps needed to move the sales cycle forward. You can use the SAP and MAP interchangeably, depending on the steps needed to close business. For example, if the prospect is not an active buyer but may become active within a certain timeframe, move the prospect into a passive marketing mode and execute the plan using the MAP as a guideline.

To close more product and service sales immediately, lay out a SAP on the first of every month, account by account.

A Sales Action Plan includes:

- The prospect's name, title, and company name

- Type of proposal (product, service, design, development, software, etc.)

- The opportunity value in dollars for the next twelve months

- The sales steps that have been completed so far and on what date

- The sales steps that need to be taken and on what date

- A list of specific help needed from management and operations to complete the sale

- A summary of the competitive environment

- A list of open issues

This process will allow you to identify any barriers that may stand in the way of closing the deal. By detailing the business opportunities you expect to close each month, you will find that your closing ratio will go up. Again, focus on premeditated steps to close sales during a specific month.

Date Management Plan

Another key ingredient in closing product and service sales is the process of *Date Management Plan.* Many salespeople present and sell to their managers on the accuracy of their sales forecasts as a predictor of new revenue. I am surprised, however, at how often experienced salespeople forecast an opportunity about to be closed without listing an expected closing date.

In my opinion, if a deal has steps that cannot be completed by the fifteenth of the month, the deal is not forecast for the month—regardless of whether the senior executive says he is making the decision *by the thirtieth* .

You must efficiently manage the twenty business days each month you have to raise your level of success. In professional sales, *time* is a competitor.

Instead of forecasting the date you *think* the sale will close, attach dates for each step needed to close the sale. This method of date management will force you to work off the steps in a planned process and close more business on time or potentially earlier.

How to Develop a Date Management Plan

1. List and describe the sales steps of your average sale.

2. As you make your first management contact, list the date of its occurrence.

3. Forecast the **next** sales steps based on your understanding of the prospect's timeline and yours.

4. Monitor your Date Management Plan weekly, making adjustments to your closing date as needed.

Date Management Plan

Month_____
Date Prepared_____
Account Manager_____

Prospect Name _____

Prospect Company _____

Proposal Type _____

Proposal Value _____

Sales Steps

Completed	Step	Date Completed or To Be Completed
Yes/No	Telephone Call	_____
Yes/No	1st Appointment	_____
Yes/No	2nd Appointment	_____
Yes/No	Product/Service Presentation	_____
Yes/No	Proposal Completed	_____
Yes/No	Proposal Submitted	_____
Yes/No	Proposal Reviewed in Person	_____
Yes/No	Proposal Negotiation	_____
Yes/No	Objections Reviewed	_____
Yes/No	Legal Reviews Contract	_____
Yes/No	Contract Signed	_____

Other Steps Needed/Help Required: _____
_____

Vendor Roadblocks: _____
_____

Competitors Involved: _____
_____

Competitive Roadblocks: _____
_____

Open Issues: _____
_____

Figure 19.   *Date Management Plan.* Use this form to plan and manage your sales cycle.

The key to closing deals faster is not focusing on the closing date, but rather on the completion dates of the various sales steps. When your forecasted sales step dates are correct, so too is your forecasted closing date.

Review and Exercises

1. Prepare a Sales Action Plan for a current opportunity. Use this to help your closing ratio go up.

2. Prepare a Date Management Plan for opportunities that are approaching the proposal stage. You can also prepare this for opportunities that are already in the proposal stage.

3. Get in the habit of preparing these two forms at the end of the week in preparation for the upcoming week or first thing Monday morning. If you prepare them on Friday, you'll have all your thoughts down and be able to enjoy your weekend. If you prepare them on Monday morning, you will want to dedicate some time earlier than you would normally start to avoid cutting into your normal workday.

Chapter 11
Managing Your Sales Cycle and Forecasting

Chapter 12

Managing Sales Objections

After reading this chapter, you will know:

- How to prepare for and respond to sales objections

- How to move a deal forward

- How to prepare for and respond to commonly received sales objections

- How to manage the prospect's perception of risk

Moving a Stalled Deal Forward

Every day professional salespeople struggle to close deals. Cold calls are not being returned, networking contacts ignore you, your proposals are being postponed, and quotas go unfulfilled. Is anybody buying anything today?

Even when market cycles are slow, companies still buy when sales reps use the *doctor* method of sales in which they heal the prospect's pain. You can gain an edge by working as a pain management specialist while your competitors take off for holiday vacation. Clients are not going to call you back if they do not believe your product or service will make them feel better.

Like a surgeon, you need to diagnose your client's issues. At the same time, you need to manage sales objection issues.

Below is a list of ten objections prospects use to stall a deal. Take your thirty- to sixty-day sales forecast and see if you can apply at least one of these ten closing bottlenecks to each of your prospects in order to better evaluate which deals to spend your sales closing time on and which deals are wasting your time.

1. Your price (or terms) is wrong.

2. My business is hurting, and you have not yet told me how to fix my pain.

3. We have no budget (no money).

4. You have not convinced me it is the right product or service.

5. You are the wrong firm and/or I don't want to work with you.

6. I am just a looker. I am not going to buy anything.

7. You are cycling me as a prospect. Can't you tell I am not interested?

8. You haven't asked me the right questions yet.

9. I am the wrong person—I have no authority to buy anything.

10. As a vendor, you are not helping me manage my risk.

To close more deals you need to focus on these ten points to understand what your current sales processes are and what needs to be changed to find prospects who will buy.

When you hear these objections, usually it means you have not communicated your business value correctly or qualified the prospect enough to understand how your product or service is priced as compared to your competition or how your product or service is a tool to drive business results. You need to evaluate what the manager is communicating to you subliminally, *not* what the words mean on the surface.

Remember this formula:

Qualified Management Buyer

+

Understanding how your product or service can fix their business pain

+

Communicate Your Value Correctly

=

No or minimal price resistance and forward movement in your sales cycle

Let's take a look at each sales objection you may hear directly or that may be implied indirectly by their actions, with a special focus on the last one, managing risk.

Your price (or terms) is wrong. To manage a price objection, just ask why the prospect believes your offering is too high. Ask them directly: *Mr./Ms. prospect, why do you believe our price is too high? As compared to what?* Remember, selling to management as a business peer gives you the right to ask direct, professionally blunt questions. Isolate the reason for their perception why they believe your product or service is too high or does not fit their needs and you can then re-educate them based on your business value and why your price is valid.

My business is hurting, and you have not yet told me how to fix my "pain." If the prospect communicates that they have a business event affecting their company, and the executive communicates uncertainty on whether he believes your product or service will resolve the event, then you have not communicated your value effectively. Prepare for this objection by developing several phrases that will better communicate your value. Develop analogies to help carry your message.

We have no budget (no money). You should always confirm the prospect has a budget in the first meeting. If they have no budget, they are not buying and you should put them in a passive marketing mode. Passive marketing will continue to put your value in front of them so when they are ready to buy, your company will already have visibility. However, as long as you are selling to a decision maker, their response about no budget may be real. To help move the sale along and further qualify the prospect, your discussion on consequence management may help them find the funding. The higher you go in the organizational chart, the less important it is to have a budget. Senior management always finds the funding if they want something.

You have not convinced me it is the right product or service. This objection comes as a result of not communicating the value of your product or service correctly. Reconfirm how your product or service will increase income, decrease expenses, or manage risks. If there are any consequences that may result from not implementing your product or service, this is the time to reconfirm those as well.

You are the wrong firm and/or I don't want to work with you. If the prospect expresses a disinterest in working with you or your firm, ask them why. Perhaps they heard something that was incorrect or possibly read something that caused them to confuse your firm with another firm. It is important to be polite and take any criticism with professional courtesy. It amazes me how many salespeople take criticism as a personal attack and suddenly become combative with the prospect. Whatever slight chances you had to change the course of the deal, will be washed away in the flood of angry dialogue. Professional salespeople take criticism (real or unfounded) and process it respectfully. If the information that the prospect has given you is incorrect, offer to provide them information from third-party sources that contradict their incorrect information. If the reason is a personal criticism, take the information and use it to better your sales skills. There may come a time when you need to call on this prospect again with a different offering or from a different company.

I am just a looker. I am not going to buy anything. Professional lookers consistently ask for marketing materials. They use your material to try to sell to their boss. The problem with this is that nine times out of ten, your marketing materials are developed for the professional looker, not for the decision maker. Marketing material is traditionally stuffed with feature and function attributes. Rarely does it communicate value that a senior executive would be intrigued by. When you find yourself conversing with a looker who is asking you for brochures, ask who will make the decision and state that you would like to forward additional information to that person. This allows you to send white papers and other items that are specifically designed to intrigue a decision maker.

You are cycling me as a prospect. Can't you tell I am not interested? Prospects are not likely to say this directly. They usually communicate this message by saying they are too busy, happy with current vendors, do not have a need for your product or service currently—anything to get you to go away and call later in hopes that you give up. Put these prospects into a passive marketing mode and start sending them information that puts your value up front. Also, take a moment to review the prospect company. Perhaps they are a healthcare facility and you are trying to sell manufacturing equipment. In this case, this prospect needs to be removed from your prospect database and replaced with a more suitable prospect.

You haven't asked me the right questions yet. This type of objection appears in the form of hedging. The prospect is usually intrigued with your sales value proposition, but cannot relate how your product or service can actually help them. If you have opened a dialogue between you and the executive, this is the time to ask direct questions. Be prepared and know their business and industry. Research their web site, research their competitors' web sites, research the industry, and be prepared to ask educated questions.

I am the wrong person—I have no authority to buy anything. Often salespeople will cycle through a database and cold call regardless of whether the contact is the right person or not just to put activity into their CRM system. This objection usually comes in the form of multiple sales meetings that never progress. If you are reaching someone who is not interested or does not have the authority to buy, you need to seek new contacts. If the prospect is a large company, this can be done by spidering several contacts. If the prospect is a small company, you should step up to the plate and ask directly who makes the decision to purchase your product or service. If they are not in a buying cycle, at least you have the name of the person who does make buying decisions.

As a vendor, you are not helping me manage my risk. Because this type of objection is prevalent, I have dedicated an entire section to it.

Managing the Prospect's Perception of Risk

Management purchases have risks involved. The prospect risks that the product or service they buy will not operate as discussed or bring about the results communicated during the pre-sales cycle. These are risks all prospects think about when evaluating you, your proposal, and your firm. As an account manager, you need to understand these issues even when they are not verbalized by the prospect.

Helping prospects manage their perception of the purchase risk will help you close more deals. In a slower economy, the risk factor increases as funding becomes tighter. Many times senior executives and presidents of small firms will not give you a risk objection. So, a key ingredient is to make sure you have communicated **proactively** to the prospect there are minimal risks dealing with your firm or using your product or service.

Do not assume that prospects know how to buy correctly. How do you discover what fears the prospect may have? It is the **what-who-why-when** questioning you ask that may result in answers. But, even more than using probing questions, you need to do an internal assessment of the issues of your firm, product, or service to determine what the risks are perceived to be. Is your firm too small? Is your product too new? Have you given sufficient client references or testimonials to make the prospect feel comfortable?

Being a small unknown company or marketing a new product or service does not mean you can't close new prospects. Think of the big-dollar deals you read about in the trades from some unknown firm who sells a Fortune 1000 company. To sell a deal like this, these companies have managed their prospect's perception of buying from an unknown vendor. They have deployed *prospect risk management* techniques.

Here are some guidelines to prepare for prospect risk management:

1. Never wait for a prospect to ask about your firm's background. Always supply details in advance. If the following variables are positive, your corporate information should include number of employees, years in business, clients' names, and annual revenue. If these variables are negative (e.g., losing money, no installations, customers hate you) then don't bring it up and just focus on the other methods listed.

2. The greater the competition, the more risk management information you must deploy to balance the prospect's perceived fear. Go after your competitor's largeness, but remember, it makes you look unprofessional if you make direct negative comments about your competition. Try to balance this with professional comments. **Always box your competitors as generalists and then talk about the category.** Do not be passive when competing against established players. It is not *who you are*; it is *who you sell against.*

3. Never have your CEO, president, or sales manager go on the first sales call. It makes your firm look small. Management executives are big guns held in reserve to be used when needed, not on the first sales call. Having management go to your first client meeting only works when your firm is a Fortune 500 and you are meeting a Fortune 500 C-level executive.

4. If you are a startup firm and have new products or services, name-drop your investor's names.

5. If you are a small or startup firm and have Fortune 1000 senior executives on your board of directors, say, "Our team includes . . ." and name-drop their positions and the companies they are associated with.

6. To manage the prospect's fear of buying something other than what was shown in a demo or overhead presentation, it is always a good idea to have a product/service sign-off sheet for any demonstration or presentation. This protects the salesperson from the prospect's demo amnesia and protects clients from being oversold.

7. When competing against big companies, manage the risk by focusing on your strengths. Use the bus analogy when competing against them: *They bus in the "A" team to sell you and the "B" team to deliver, while our team stays throughout the relationship.*

8. Never communicate your firm is a generalist. Always be a specialist. Generalist firms are always perceived to be large and slow. Specialist firms are perceived to be more customer-centric and small.

Sales objections are just roadblocks that salespeople have forgotten to get directions for before they hit their destination.- Anonymous

Manage your prospect's perception of their risk better and you will manage your sale.

Review and Exercises

1. Write down the top ten objections prospects use to stall your closings.

2. Analyze each objection and determine which objections are based on value communicated, qualification of prospect, timing not right, and risk.

   a. For the objections that fall under value communicated, review what value was not communicated effectively. Perhaps you need to reword your value based on more specific industry words or business pains.

   b. For the objections that fall under qualification of prospect, take a look at their title and make sure they are directors or above. If not, you should be contacting the decision maker.

   c. For those objections falling under timing not right, put them into a passive marketing mode. Make sure that you contact them regularly with passive marketing materials so that when the prospect is ready to buy, your company will already be in front of them.

d. For those objections falling under risk, determine what risk is perceived and craft a response to manage their risk perception.

Chapter 13

Using Storytelling as a Business Sales Tool

After reading this chapter, you will know:

- Why storytelling works

- How to develop your story

- How to provide an experience for your prospect through your story

- What components are needed to convey value

If your goal is to become a peer in the boardroom, instead of a vendor waiting in the hallway, use storytelling techniques as a tool for your success. Storytelling is defined by many as a process of relating images, anecdotes, and visual associations so the receiver can relate to the information being supplied.

When used correctly, storytelling breaks down the prospect's perception of you being a salesperson and opens the door for them to see you as an advisor. Storytelling has been around as long as men and women have been on this earth. In ancient times, when much of the world's population was illiterate, fables and myths were used to create visual brochures in the heads of listeners on different ideas and philosophies that were being communicated.

The goal of executive storytelling is to communicate value by relating business anecdotes so the buyer can experience the value of what you are selling. When prospects experience the value of your product or service, it is called **experiential selling**. This multi-dimensional method of communication helps prospects use all of their senses as you describe the specific sales value proposition for your product or service. Because of this multi-sensory selling process, your closing ratio will increase because it subliminally communicates to prospects that you are like them.

Executive storytelling is not just a case study. It is a personal communication method with a peer that creates a human emotional environment with some point of view. As a salesperson, you can use executive storytelling in direct mail, on the telephone, during an electronic web presentation, and in person—though in-person is always preferred.

Although business storytelling uses some of the standard foundation and approaches of regular storytelling, it also uses a different format. Storytelling helps management prospects understand your firm and build trust with you personally. It helps you earn the right to sell them.

Why does executive storytelling work?

- ▶ It gives salespeople broader freedom to describe their products or services in a non-traditional way instead of using structured brochures, electronic presentations, or technical specifications.

- ▶ It allows executives to see issues through their peer's experiences before they buy from you and reduces their fear of making an incorrect vendor selection.

- ▶ It provides inspiration for executive prospects to buy based on emotion and impression.

As discussed before, using your company's brand can interfere with the visual brochure you are trying to create. In storytelling, never use your company brand as a storytelling feature.

Building Your Executive Storytelling Format

1. When you develop your story, make sure you have a written goal and message you want to communicate to the executive. Select five or six

specific points you wish to convey and create a
unique story for each (e.g., how they made their
decision story, price story, value story, etc.).

2. Keep each story short. Less than seven
    paragraphs.

3. Always name any market research sources or
    statistics you quote or use in your story.

4. Make the story specifically relevant to the exact
    conversation you are having or the information
    you are trying to educate the prospect on.

5. When developing your story, use unique or
    unusual words and descriptions during your
    conversation so the prospect will remember the
    story and it will stand out (e.g., the bus story,
    the storm story, etc.).

6. Give life to inanimate objects for use as
    business analogies (e.g., the sponge story, the
    glass window story, etc.).

7. Write all of your stories down. Remember
    selling to management is premeditated. Plan,
    practice, and present and it will sound natural.

8. Use your executive dictionary during your
    storytelling and try to use ten words per story

that are relevant to the executive you are talking with.

9. Name a place, day of the week, and geography in your storytelling. This technique brings your story to life.

Personalizing Your Business Story

Once you have developed your story, you will want to personalize it with the following attributes:

1. Always use the prospect's first name when telling them a story.

2. When possible, if you are telling a story about another client who may use your product or service, try to use their first name in the story.

3. Always use the word *we* to imply company depth.

4. Use adjectives to give the story visual depth.

5. Always use the word *specialist* to describe your firm, never the word *expert*. As I mentioned in an earlier chapter, the word *expert* implies legal certification that may have to be proven.

6. Use action verbs in your story to send subliminal messages to the prospect that they need to take action.

Example: Generic Story

We offer a broad range of programs and services. Recently the XYZ Company had some of the same objections you do but after they made an in-depth study, they decided to go with us instead of the competition.

Example: Value Forward Selling Storytelling

Recently, John Smith of the XYZ Company had some of the same objections you have. John, who is the CFO for the company, is headquartered out of their Boston office and manages multiple divisional groups for their firm. John and his team decided to do a detailed, exhaustive study of which company in our industry has the more reliable and cost-effective offerings.

After their ninety-day business review, John called us and said that he wanted to go with us because he believed our product (or service) would help his team increase their corporate profits by at least 20% this year.

John also said that once they used our product, they actually underestimated how easy it was to use.

Storytelling is an advanced sales skill that can be used at any step of your sales cycle. Develop a broad range of stories based on targeted goals you wish to accomplish during your sales process and you will sell more. Make sure you develop a sales story for every sales step.

Chapter 13
Using Storytelling as a Business Sales Tool

Review and Exercises

1. Create five to ten stories based on what you sell using the top sales objections you hear from prospects (i.e., price story, delivery story, etc.).

2. Make a list of actual case studies with current or previous customers. Build a story on each case study.

Chapter 13
Using Storytelling as a Business Sales Tool

Chapter 14

Managing Your Competition

After reading this chapter, you will know:

- Who you *really* sell against

- How to craft your value to stand out from your competition

- Why people in your own firm may be considered your competitor

- Why your competition does not always have to be a tangible person or firm

It's Not Who You Are—It's Who You Sell Against

For more than twenty years, I have successfully sold products and services against major Fortune 1000 companies in North America. In many cases, the firms I worked for, or consulted with, were the new player on the block or the small up-and-coming player taking on all newcomers or mature firms in the declining stage of their company life cycle.

If, on a daily basis, you are losing more business to competitors than winning, it's more than likely not so much the fault of your employer's product or service as the sales techniques you use.

Harsh words, but more than likely, they are true.

We all have competitors.

The key is to treat your competitors like a Navy Seal would treat the enemy. In the sales world, it's kill or be killed. Statistically, once the agreement is signed with another firm, your opportunity to successfully close additional business with that client is minimal.

First, let's define who your competitors are. Competitors include any firm or person who prevents you from closing a contract with your targeted executive. Based on this definition, your competitors could be your own operations or finance department, the companies you sell against regionally, or some national player who has great trade press.

If you have been selling products or services long enough, you will have lost major deals and commissions because your own firm did not respond expeditiously or correctly to a business opportunity.

I am not talking about the wild deals we all come across from time to time that don't fit our existing product or service definitions. I am talking about clean deals where operations, finance, engineering, or your management team could not deliver the requested help you needed to close the big deal.

Let's be frank. They are your competitors. And, if you ignore these internal competitors, you will not be as successful as you should be.

The key is *to never negatively sell*, but to offensively sell to put your competition in a defensive position.

In professional sales, it is not what you sell—it is who you sell against.

Dealing With Competitors—Kill or be Killed

After regularly selling against many public Fortune 1000 firms and established private firms, I developed tools that allow me to succeed against the big guys. Let's review my competitive tools:

- Use your sales value proposition as a weapon. It should fight off some of the bigger players that are really generalists. Always box your competition (no matter how big they are) as generalists and then position yourself as a specialist. Management always buys from specialists.

- When selling against known competitors, make a list of the top ten questions the prospect should ask all vendors. Structure the list so it highlights your firm's strengths and your competitors' weaknesses and then send it to your client as part of your Touch Management Program. Focus on consequence management. What are the consequences if your management prospect buys from the wrong company?

- Never assume there are no competitors. *There are always competitors.*

- When dealing with large national firms, always stress your local presence.

- When competitors are in the hunt for your deal, always have the practice manager or operations manager responsible for deploying your product or services meet the management executives personally.

- Do not sell negatively. Never mention a competitor by name when you are describing company differences. Always paint a big picture (e.g., big five companies, companies with international offices, companies that use third-party support, etc.).

- Always make sure your firm does competitive reviews. Knowing who you're selling against provides you with the means to keep closing deals.

Case Study—Managing Competition: Top Seven Questions

Several years ago, I was in a trade show booth surrounded by competitors. All of these players were more established firms. Having done a business case review on all of their feature sets, I knew their products' weaknesses. To protect our turf and to create a more level playing field at the show, I created the "**Top Seven Questions**" list you should ask every vendor at the show. My sales team and I handed this list to every prospect who walked into our booth. The list contained no competitor names. It was just general questions that highlighted our business strengths and our competitors' weaknesses.

During the show, prospects would walk into our competitor's booths, hold our list in their hand, and grill them on their answers.

One of the questions was about our firm's sales value proposition. Our competitors could not know what it was, of course, because I had made it up only two weeks before.

Was it successful? Yes.

Was it hunter warfare? Yes.

In Value Forward Selling, it is kill or be killed.

Types of Competition

Competitors are born on a daily basis. To succeed, it's important to identify who your competitors are and what their weaknesses are.

1. Your Own Company's Employees (Internal Competitors)

It is sad to say, but if you are a five-person professional service or product shop or a 3,000-person major corporate player, on a day-to-day basis, you have to deal with internal competition in your company. Such internal competition stands in the way of closing more sales and increasing your income. You cannot ignore it. It will not go away. The only way to deal with it is by identifying where the roadblocks are and putting a system in place for management of these internal impediments.

For large sales organizations (over 1,000 employees), managing internal competitors is more difficult due to the installed corporate bureaucracy. The easiest method to deal with departments that stand in your way is to use your regional VP or national vice president of sales as your advocate. You need to document how each department's inability to be sales-driven has affected your business sales. List examples of how the specific department did not follow up with a prospect or you on specific questions in a timely manner, or how the department failed to update the new proposal template describing your firm's new service or product capabilities that would have put you on the short list of vendors. **All of these causes need to be documented.**

To succeed over your internal competitors, document and submit this information to your sales management team. They have more bullets in their pistols, which gives them more opportunities to fix these issues without you being shot by your corporate vice president.

If you work for a small company, you have a greater opportunity to directly influence the internal competition issue. Again, document what happens and go through your sales management team to resolve the issues. If the vice president of sales is too busy or too weak, set up a meeting directly with the vice president of the department you are having problems with to show how lost revenue opportunities hurt them just like they hurt you.

2. Your Prospects' Existing Vendors

If you are aggressively using your sales value proposition to get meetings and you are calling on VPs and above only, more than likely your prospect is either not happy with their existing vendors or your sales value proposition is so intriguing that the company will consider you anyway. Remember, senior executives do not like to waste time, so if you have a meeting, they are interested. They may also be unhappy with their current vendor, but are not likely to tell you.

The difference between management and supervisors is that management values their time more than you do. If you meet with supervisors, they will waste your time even when they are happy with their current vendors.

3. New Competitors Proposing Simultaneously

This is the real business world. Nothing is easy. To beat competitors, continue to be different. Focus on your sales value proposition and the fact that you are a specialist. When describing your competitors, always refer to them as generalists and yourself as a specialist.

You can win major deals by stressing this difference. Since management buys based on impression, not on features, price, or function, this competitor management technique (specialists versus generalists) helps buyers visualize your difference and your value.

4. National Product or Service Competitors That Your Prospect Is Going to Call

One of the easiest ways to beat large established competitive players is using storytelling techniques. When selling to management, always use stories to personalize your conversations. More than case studies, storytelling helps management visualize the point you are trying to make. Many times business case studies are tool structured and impersonal in their communications approach . But storytelling humanizes the visual impression to management that you are a peer. Case studies are used by vendors; storytelling is used by peers. Use this technique and you will win deals over your competitor.

5. Your Prospect's Decision Influencers

There is no question that other decision-influencing supervisors inside your prospect's company can be your competitors. Supervisors are professional lookers. To deal with this situation effectively, confront it before it gets out of control. If you are using this program correctly, you will deal with the decision makers directly. In bypassing lower-level decision influencers, you should expect some internal politics and jealousy. But, as soon as the decision maker identifies the decision influencers to you, you need to placate their egos and get them involved in the cycle of your sale. When selling to Fortune 1000 companies, the more allies and points of entry you have, the better.

Always manage supervisors based on their needs, but never sell to them.

Review and Exercises

1. Make a list of your competitors and segment the list by your own company's employees, the prospect's existing vendors, external competitors the prospect may call or is already talking with, and the prospect's decision-influencers.

   a. In your own company, determine how you can manage this competition more effectively.

   b. As for the prospect's existing vendors, you should study their weaknesses and develop your value around their weaknesses. Remember, many prospects don't buy from existing vendors a second time.

   c. When it comes to external competitors, again, study their weaknesses and your strengths. Develop talking points on how your product or service will increase income, decrease expenses, or manage risks in comparison to your competitors' weaknesses.

   d. Determine if you are dealing with decision influencers in the prospect company. If so, manage their needs and you will see your competition erode.

Chapter 14
Managing Your Competition

Chapter 15

Following Up After the Sale

After reading this chapter, you will know:

- Why follow-up is crucial to developing a relationship with a prospect

- How to manage post-sale consequences

Developing a Relationship with Your Client

Selling prospects is not a one-time event. As discussed, the first sale to a prospect is a transactional sale. Of course, the goal is to get more sales from your prospect and move your first interaction from a transactional sale to a relationship sale.

To achieve recurring sales with the same prospect, however, you must follow through after the first sale to help the prospect see the value you described during the pre-sale process.

Like management prospects, we are all buyers. Our hope is that as soon as we buy, we do not regret our decision. To help your prospect experience the value they bought, it is critical that you follow up with the management buyer directly during the post-sales timeline.

Never expect your support team, customer service team, or your operations team to be the liaison with your client. It is your job as a professional salesperson to interact with your new customer to help them maximize the expectations sold to them during the sales cycle and to help them manage their fear of buyer consequences.

Action Steps to Take After the First Sale

1. Depending on the value of the sale, after the sale has been completed, schedule an on-site meeting or a teleconference call with the customer to review what they bought in detail and its current fulfillment of their business needs. Make sure your first call is not a sales call or a networking request, because this will diminish the effect of your follow-up call.

2. At your meeting, bring the list of objectives the prospect described as their goals during the pre-sales program and review it in your post-sales meeting.

3. Make a list of variances described by the buyer based on what they think they received and what they think they bought and review the differences.

4. Discuss how you (and your firm) can close the gap between any differences.

To move your prospect from a transactional customer to a relationship customer, you must bridge the gaps between perception of purchase and reality of delivery. Customers only buy more than once when the pre-sales cycle conversation delivers the post-sales cycle expectations.

Professional salespeople learn how to manage this by understanding clearly the prospect's buying reasons during pre-sales and documenting those expectations to deliver during the post-sales follow-up.

Relationship sales only happen when you make them happen.

Chapter 15
Following Up After the Sale

Review and Exercises

1. Review what type of follow-up you have provided to clients in the past. Did you call them to find out if they have any questions or need assistance?

2. Develop a plan of action to follow-up with clients. Implement this plan of action with your current clients.

Chapter 15
Following Up After the Sale

Chapter 16

Making a Difference with Business Ethics

After reading this chapter, you will know:

- Why salespeople are often misjudged

- How you can improve communications with a prospect

- What the responsibilities of the buyer are

Understanding Why Ethics Is Important

After a conversation with a senior vice president of a Fortune 100 company, I decided to end this book with a chapter on ethics. It seems that the importance of ethics in business would be obvious to any professional; but as communicated by the senior VP, there is an issue with some salespeople who are not ethically motivated during the sales process or after-sales support.

I am not naïve. I understand there are salespeople who lie, deceive, and fraudulently misrepresent their product, service, or company's capabilities during the pre-sales process to get the commission.

Of course, this is unacceptable. As a profession, it is important for all of us to build business respect with prospects—both pre- and post-sales—that helps them see the value communicated and ultimately delivered. As a professional salesperson, you are immediately subjected to the biased assumptions that some buyers have based on their last interaction with another salesperson. This negative attitude is to some degree earned depending on your industry, but usually represents a minority rather than a majority of sales representatives of that business market.

Salespeople who are unscrupulous are focused on the short-term. Yes, they may generate some sales, but their reputation and success is usually short-lived.

However, to be fair to the sales profession, sometimes prospects do not know how to buy and then they blame salespeople for the misperceptions of what they expected to get versus what they received.

Responsibility of the Buyer

Depending on what the product or service is, smart buyers check references, use legal intermediaries to review contracts, and do their own internal due diligence prior to signing a contract. Additionally, it is important that buyers understand the consequences for implementing, maintaining, or deploying their purchase.

Selling involves both the buyer and the seller. We need our profession to be more professional and we need prospects to be better buyers.

To be a great salesperson, you must sell and deliver your trust to prospects. Selling wholesale supplies that are short-shipped, jewelry that is underweight, software that is not ready, or truckloads of building supplies that are flawed usually comes back to affect your ability to build trust and directly affects your sales commissions and future sales.

Sales professionals sell trust as an invisible value.

Chapter 16
Making a Difference with Business Ethics

Review and Exercises

1. Take a look at the industry you are in. Is there a perception of unethical sales practices? If so, prepare yourself for being prejudged by a prospect. To help reduce the immediate conclusion a prospect may come to, be creative and approach your prospect in a more professional manner. Perhaps the industry as a whole approaches sales with the same method of attack. If you are creative and approach it from a different angle, you may be able to penetrate accounts that might not have otherwise taken your call.

Chapter 16
Making a Difference with Business Ethics

Conclusion

By its very nature, selling products and services to management is a difficult and cumbersome task. On a daily basis, salespeople carry a yoke around their necks—it's called a sales quota (or sales target). It pays well to those who succeed . . . and chokes those who fail.

One of the unique nuances of professional sales is that the lifetime value of an original sale can become a multiplier opportunity generating large commissions for salespeople over and over.

But, for any sales executive to be consistently successful, there are important business ethics that need to be practiced on a regular business.

Today, Fortune 1000 management executives and presidents of privately held firms seek long-term relationships with vendors. This need is based on the bad reputation many firms and salespeople have earned during the last ten years. This reputation has been developed based on the lack of financial capabilities of many companies from the '90s and the inability of vendors to deliver the product or service that was sold.

With this ever-present buyer perception, it is doubly important that as a professional salesperson you communicate your firm's capabilities with honesty and interact with the management prospect in an honorable and accurate way.

To sell more to management, build trust.

To sell more, build long-term relationships that start after the second sale.

Long-term business relationships not only help you in a current sales cycle, but also allow you to move from your current position into new opportunities by providing a base of existing contacts who will help launch your new sales position quicker. To build long-term relationships, you must get past the first sale and sell what you have, not what you wish you had!

By reading this book, you've learned the successful tactics, practices, and vernacular to be a more successful salesperson. You may have learned concepts and ideas that were new or challenging to your established sales training experiences. Becoming a peer in the boardroom, instead of a vendor waiting in the hallway takes practice, patience, and skill; it is a learned process that Value Forward Selling gives you.

To help you see these concepts in practice, I have relayed to you actual experiences I encountered during my past and present sales tenure. My firm also offers on-site marketing, sales, strategy development, and sales training. If you would like our team to customize our methods to your business needs, please contact us.

At the end of this chapter is a sixty-day action plan. Follow through on this plan and you should see a dramatic increase in your sales commissions.

Thanks for your support, and please let me know about your sales successes and how I can help you become a hunter!

Hunt now, or be eaten later!

Paul R. DiModica
paul@pauldimodica.com

Conclusion

APPENDIX A

Sixty-Day Value Forward Selling Action Plan

The following is a strategic and tactical deployment blueprint to help you increase your product or service sales and propel your revenue upward. This is the *actual* sales development plan I've used to help launch successful product and service companies. You may use all of it or any segment you deem appropriate to help increase your sales. Depending on your budget, your personal goals, and your needs, this plan can be accelerated or elongated in time. The Value Forward Selling Action Plan will produce customer leads, sales opportunities, and quick market identification for you and your business.

Week One

- Start creating your sales value proposition.

- Determine your top ten prospects in each of the verticals your firm sells to. Visit their web sites and print out ten pages from each site.

- Circle the common words and messages expressed on each of these web sites.

- Write down multiple sales value proposition examples. Be creative. Seek to produce at least twenty prototypes for review.

- Start to plan your executive seminar series. Shoot for your first date to be eight weeks from today. Pick a topic.

- Select five sales value proposition examples from your master list of twenty. Test them out on your co-workers. Select one that best positions your company as being a specialist.

- Start designing your marketing materials to match your new sales value proposition.

- Start writing your new sales value proposition's telemarketing script.

- Start designing a postcard that highlights your sales value proposition.

Week Two

- Update your web site's home page with your sales value proposition.

- Finish your postcard design. Send it to the printer.

- Finish your marketing collateral design. Send it to the printer.

- Select the venue for your seminar series. Choose a facility that can hold 150 people comfortably. Contact the venue and reserve four dates over four months.

- Write down the top ten sales objections for each product and service you sell. Start creating white papers based on the titles and verticals of the person who gave you the sales objections.

- Try out your new sales value proposition telemarketing script on your work associates. Develop your objection management script to accompany the telemarketing script.

- Develop your executive dictionary of terms to use with your management prospects based on their vertical industry and specific titles.

- Select a business book to send to management executives. Review the book to confirm there is no objectionable material inside.

- Create a list of fifty companies and/or executives you want to send the book to.

- Meet with associated strategic partners and ask them to speak at one of your four upcoming seminars.

Week Three

- Inspect the seminar location to confirm fit and size. Sign the agreement.

- Start telemarketing your new sales value proposition to management executives. Shoot for thirty new cold calls a day. (Stockbrokers do 100 a day.) Set up meetings.

- Purchase fifty books to send to your prospects.

- Design an invitation with an RSVP (like a wedding invitation) for your upcoming seminar. Include all four dates on the invitation. Send it to the printer.

- Attend one evening networking function.

Week Four

- Pick up your completed marketing materials, postcard, and seminar invitations.

- Mail seminar invitations to 2,000 prospects, existing and past clients, and the press.

- Mail fifty books to management prospects.

- Continue calling every day. Set up meetings.

- Submit seminar outline to partner speakers.

- Create an "Executive Sponsorship" overview to sell sponsorships for your executive seminars. Sell them at $12,000 for each seminar or $40,000 for all four.

Week Five

- Keep calling. Set up meetings.

- Contact the fifty management executives who received the book and set up a meeting.

- Mail 1,000 postcards to management executives.

- Cold call partners to sell seminar sponsorships.

- Place an advertisement in the business section of your local Sunday paper about the upcoming seminar. Make sure the advertisement identifies the title you are seeking to draw to the seminar.

- Request twenty questions from each seminar speaker to review.

- Contact editors of local papers to have lunch and talk about your business seminar series.

- Attend one networking function. Invite all management contacts to the seminar.

Week Six

- Keep calling. Set up meetings.

- Send out another 2,000 invitations to the same management executives. This will be their second invitation.

- Attend two networking functions.

Week Seven

- Keep calling. Set up meetings.

- Meet with your seminar presenters to go through the format.

- Send out RSVP confirmations to seminar registrants.

- Mail out 2,000 postcards to management executives.

- Attend two networking functions.

Week Eight

- Keep calling. Set up meetings.

- Attend one networking function.

- Hold your seminar.

- Mail out fifty more books to new management prospects.

- After the first seminar, mail out 2,000 invitations to the next seminar.

- Meet with new speakers for the second seminar.

- Meet with local press for lunch. Pitch a story.

Appendix A

APPENDIX B

Lead Generation and Management

Database Contact Lists:

Hoover's Online   www.hoovers.com

Dun & Bradstreet   www.dnb.com

ZapData   www.zapdata.com

Database Contact Management:

SalesForce.com   www.salesforce.com

SalesLogix   www.saleslogix.com

Appendix B

APPENDIX C

Example Forms

First Meeting Talking Points	
Date Prepared:	
Sales Rep:	
Client's Name:	
Contacts:	
Business Type:	
Public/Private:	
# of Employees:	
Business URL:	
Industry Business Pains:	
Industry Terminology:	
Sales value proposition to communicate:	
Our Associates Talking Points:	
Areas to Avoid:	
Meeting Goals:	
Goal Time Period:	
Potential Purchase:	
Value of Deal:	
Additional Comments:	

Three Box Monty™
Presentation Format
Length: 1 - 1½ hours

Team Prep	**Minutes**
• Presenter group arrives at least 30 minutes early. Meets in parking lot.	30

Presentation

1.	Presenter introductions/business cards are handed out.	--
2.	Attendees' introductions.	5
3.	Lead presenter (salesperson) confirms the amount of time available for the presentation.	
4.	Lead presenter reconfirms the business pains expressed by the management contact coupled with industry pains.	5
5.	Lead presenter launches into slide presentation (8 slides or less) giving company history, client list, and sales value proposition.	10
6.	Three Box Monty™ presentation (depending on if you have a product or specialized service to explain).	15-30
7.	Optional step: Service or product presenter launches into physical demo of product or service that is being sold. If not applicable, move on to Step 8.	
8.	Executive Briefing Close Client Q and A. Wrap-up. Ask transactional questions of senior executives to confirm they are still qualified.	10

Client Negotiation Form

Client Name_____ Date _____

Client Contact_____ Title_____

Account Manager_____

1. Why will the management prospect buy from us? What's their business pain?_

_____

2. Why will we lose the deal? _____

_____

3. What are the top ten expected sales objections we anticipate to hear from the decision-making team? _____

_____

_____

4. What is the political environment of the decision? _____

_____

5. What does your firm have to do to close this sale and to meet the prospect's personal and business needs? _____

_____

6. What are the business consequences that the prospect is exposed to if they do not buy at all, or they buy from another competitor whose product or service does not fix their business pain? _____

_____

7. What is their stated budget for your product or service?_____

_____

Date Management Plan

Month_____
Date Prepared_____
Account Manager_____

Prospect Name _____
Prospect Company _____

Proposal Type _____
Proposal Value _____

Sales Steps

Completed	Step	Date Completed or To Be Completed
Yes/No	Telephone Call	_____
Yes/No	1st Appointment	_____
Yes/No	2nd Appointment	_____
Yes/No	Product/Service Presentation	_____
Yes/No	Proposal Completed	_____
Yes/No	Proposal Submitted	_____
Yes/No	Proposal Reviewed in Person	_____
Yes/No	Proposal Negotiation	_____
Yes/No	Objections Reviewed	_____
Yes/No	Legal Reviews Contract	_____
Yes/No	Contract Signed	_____

Other Steps Needed/Help Required: _____
_____
_____

Vendor Roadblocks: _____
_____

Competitors Involved: _____
_____

Competitive Roadblocks: _____
_____

Open Issues: _____
_____
_____

[Your Company Name]
[Your Sales Value Proposition]

Presentation Talking Points Form

Lead Presenter's Name (salesperson):_____

Client's name_____

Client's URL_____

Client's Address/Briefing Location_____

Briefing Date_____Briefing Time_____

Time Allocated to Briefing by Client_____

Meeting Lead Attendee:

Name_____   Title_____

Meeting Attendees:

Name_____   Title_____

Name_____   Title_____

Name_____   Title_____

Client's Pain Issues_____

Product or Service To Be Presented_____

Presenter's Name

Title_____

Responsible for Presentation Slide (List slide number/subject)_____

Presenter's Name

Title_____

Responsible for Presentation Slide (List slide number/subject)_____

Presenter's Name

Title_____

Responsible for Slide/Whiteboard Presentation (List slide number/subject)_____

Goal of Presentation_____

What does the prospect want to see/hear at the meeting?_____

Current product/service being used by the prospect_____

Current business pain with existing product or service_____

What do we want to sell them?_____

What is the dollar value for the first year?_____

What is the dollar value of this client over the next three years?_____

Do they have a budget?   _____Yes   _____No   If yes, how much?___

When do they want this product or service?_____

Why will they buy from us?_____

Why will we lose this deal?_____

Which contact is signing the purchase order/contract?_____

Which contact(s) is (are) making the decision?_____

Is there a consultant involved?   _____Yes   _____No
    If yes, what is the consultant's name?_____
    Consultant's company name_____
    Consultant's telephone_____
    Is the consultant: For us_____ Against us_____ Neutral_____

What are the prospect's business consequences if they do not buy from us?_____

What does the selling team need to do to close this business?_____

Are there any unusual marketing expenses needed to close this business?_____

Next Action Steps_____

Appendix C

Index

Other Services and Publications by Paul DiModica

Free Weekly Sales Strategy Newsletter
BDM News
www.bdmnews.com

BDM News is the world's largest online magazine for sales and marketing executives in growth directed firms. Weekly get free tips on sales, strategy and marketing techniques to increase your sales success. BDM New is read in over 110 countries.

DigitalHatch Services
www.digitalhatch.com

Paul DiModica offers value forward sales and marketing services to clients seeking to increase corporate revenue including:

- Event Speaking
- Sales and Marketing Strategy Development and Consulting
- Executive Coaching
- Team Sales Training

Sales Management Power Strategies
Available at www.digitalhatch.com

A sales management publication designed to help executives build a replicable and scalable sales process for their team. This book includes:

- How to calculate lost sales analysis to understand true sales territory potential by geography
- Discover the mathematical formula to correctly calculate sales team quotas every time
- Learn the top 15 sales team metrics you need to monitor to increase your revenue capture success
- **The 8 most common types of salespeople and how to hire the right outbound sales team members** who succeed and fit with your company's current sales business model needs
- How to <u>turn you team into successful quota salespeople</u> without getting an ulcer
- How to use strategic and alliance partners to **generate more sales,** not just press releases
- How to manage salespeople who work in virtual offices
- How to set up and implement a **Sales Scorecard** to monitor corporate business development performance that generates increased revenue
- What interview questions you must ask (and most managers don't) to hire the right salesperson for your team
- The number one place to find experienced, industry-specific salespeople at almost no cost

- A step-by-step guide on how to build a replicable and scalable sales team process that works with both new and experienced sales team members
- How to hold sales meetings that increase your sales team's performance and their appreciation of your mentorship
- The <u>eight most important steps</u> needed to integrate the entire organization into an outbound sales and business development machine
- How to build a sales compensation program that manages sales team member's behavior and motivates them to sell more

Printed in the United States
49544LVS00001BD/70-255